ETHNICITY IN NORTH EAST INDIA

ETHNICITY IN NORTH EAST INDIA

Sarthak Sengupta

GYAN

ISBN : 978-81-212-1216-8

Price: ₹ 550

First Published, 2014

Published by

Gyan Publishing House
23, Main Ansari Road, Darya Ganj,
New Delhi-110002
Ph. : 23282060, 23261060
E-mail: books@gyanbooks.com

Laser Typesetting : Sanya Computers, Delhi
Printed at : G. Print Process, Delhi

Cataloging in Publication Data—DK

Courtesy: D.K. Agencies (P) Ltd. <docinfo@dkagencies.com>

Ethnicity in North East India / Sarthak Sengupta.

p. cm.
Contributed articles.
Includes bibliographical references and index.
ISBN 9788121212168

1. Ethnicity—India, Northeastern. I. Sengupta, Sarthak, 1955-

DDC 305.8009541 23

Dedicated
to the cherished memory of
my elder sister
Late Supti Dasgupta

Contents

Preface

The concept of ethnicity is very much linked with the issue of identity and also linked with aspect of culture. Ethnicity is an accepted state of mankind. It is one of the most common ways in which people announce and assert their individuality by maxim who they are or who they are not. In contemporary world however, with mounting inter-dependence and contact among the international group of people, there seems to be a kind of expansion of the limits of the accredited humankind. However, despite the various forces of globalisation, issues relating to ethnicity, may be in wide-ranging forms, seem to continue as a universal predicament. The problem becomes more challenging when it is coupled with violence and militancy.

In contemporary social science research, one finds increasing use of the terms like ethnic identity; ethnicity to refer to 'community level consciousness and solidarity'. The term 'ethnicity' first appeared in Oxford English Dictionary in 1972, and in American Heritage Dictionary in 1973, but, perhaps used for the first time in 1953. The word ethnic group, derived etymologically from the Greek word *'ethnos'*, originally meant a race or a primitive culture or autochthonous group or a tribe or a nation. According to Oxford Dictionary, ethnic pertains to race originating from a specified racial, linguistic and cultural group, usually a minority group. The members entertain a conviction in their common descent; and a sense of common distinctiveness and belongingness.

Constituents of an ethnic group may distinguish themselves base on certain common physical-cultural characteristics. An ethnic group may sometimes be interchangeably used to refer to a nationality, minority, a tribe, a community, a culture, a society, a race, a people or a nation. It does not matter whether or not objective blood relationship exists among them. Ethnic groups are usually categories of ascription, the credentials of which are made by the actors themselves. However, more often than not such identity of individuals and/or groups alter outline in consonance with socio-cultural contexts as well as over a period of time. In fact, an individual or a group can possess quite a few identities, latent or apparent, concurrently, but projects one that according to the self-assessment of individuals or groups may appear proper in the specific situation.

Ethnicity is seen to be very closely related with the demands of identity formation of an ethnic group and is usually 'viewed as a device as much as a focus of group mobilisation by the leadership of ethnic group through select use of ethnic symbols for socio-cultural and politico-economic purpose'. Ethnic cohesion as well as we feeling is actually created through social and political processes, especially in the context of competition for scarce resources.

North East India, popularly known as seven sisters, comprises the States of Assam, Arunachal Pradesh, Manipur, Meghalaya, Mizoram, Nagaland and Tripura. For administrative purpose, of late, Sikkim has also been included in North East India. The region is considered as cultural corridor between India and South East Asia, and has a tremendous strategical importance, not only because of its geography but also because of its history, demography and culture. The region provides shelter to numerous peoples of various ethnic affiliation having different social structures, cultural heritages and cultural linkages across the international borders. There is a rich assembly of cultures and communities in the rugged expanse of the eastern Himalayas. Connected with the main body of the country by a narrow strip of land, sharing four international borders and having cultural linkages with trans-Himalayan societies, North East India has shot into limelight in the recent decades owing to a series of ethnic-cultural movements, mostly reflecting sub-national sentiments.

The North Eastern region, in fact, is too diverse a region and each State or sub-national group which is today in the hang on of insurgent politics has a distinct history and culture of its own. Apart from socio-economic and political factors, socio-historical and cultural factors have also been acting as strong propellants for these movements and until these factors are understood in their proper context it would be difficult to judge the mind-set of the participants of the diverse ethnic organisations, belligerent or otherwise.

Recently, several numerically diminutive and politically weaker tribes in North East India have shown a preference for identity shifts and creating new alliances or intensification of olden ties. There is substantial flexibility in the state of affairs. Efforts of changing identity in most of the cases depend upon the prevailing ethno-political situation. With regard to ethnic alignment, in Manipur, there have been several cases of shift from the Kuki to the Naga axis in recent years, but without changing their ethnic boundary.

The understanding of identity dynamics in North East India is important because innumerable social problems are associated with it. Since Independence, some of the major challenges to the process of nation-building in India have occurred in the north eastern region of the country. While some of the movements have aimed at the creation of autonomous States within the Indian Union, some are aspiring to be included under Sixth Schedule; some are demanding for inclusion in the Scheduled Tribe category; others have been demanding separation from the country. In most cases the Indian States have succeeded in accommodating the peoples' demands within the ambit of the Constitution. But, there are still certain organisations which have been able to plead for a large measure of support from the people, for their pro-independence agenda.

The study of ethnicity has been a major passion of anthropology and other branches of social sciences of contemporary times. Ethnicity is not a simple and isolable social occurrence, rather interconnected to many other multifaceted societal issues. Examining and understanding ethnicity requires multiple dimensions as it operates and channelise through various ways and means. Social scientists generally tend to look for the genesis of ethnic movements within the structure of the society and one theory discernible in such an explanation is that of relative deprivation and collective bargaining. However, the theory of relative deprivation which holds that one group considers itself to be deprived in relation to the group (class) in the position of rulers and therefore resorts to conflict (revolution) as a tactic of their movement in order to establish a new order in society may not always be sufficient by itself to generate a movement of the type that exists in the north eastern States of India.

Although dynamic nature of ethnicity has attracted attention of large number of scholars, hardly any serious attempt has been made to understand the mechanism according to which the character of its transient solidarity becomes manifest. Ethnicity as an area of anthropological enquiry is yet to receive adequate attention in this remote corner of our country.

It is hoped that the present compilation will contribute in a small measure towards a better understanding of the problem of peoples' hostility in all its diverse aspects and help in approaching the entire issue in its proper perspectives.

1st February, 2014 **Sarthak Sengupta**

Acknowledgements

I owe a special debt of thankfulness to all the contributors to this volume for their enthusiasm to co-operate in this endeavour and wish to thank the very many colleagues who supported and stimulated me to make this exercise possible. The articles included have highlighted and questions the issues of ethnicity and ethnic identity in North East India critically with sources and genesis of the movements.

It has been possible for me to continue my academic pursuit because of the infrastructural facilities provided by the authorities of Dibrugarh University. The university, colleagues and students provided me excellent support. I avail of this opportunity to express my thanks. I wish to acknowledge the wonderful secretarial support of Mrs Neelanjana Barua. She typed the manuscript with incredible speed and precision and with remarkable zeal and skill. She deserves special commendation. Special thank goes to Dr Dali Dutta, whose unwavering support was so very much appreciated.

As always my wife, Kaveeta; my sons Sushruta and Samrat; and my daughter-in-law Surovee have been uncomplaining, compassionate and in good spirits all the way through the always arduous progression of understanding, re-writing and editing involved in the compilation of this treatise. I am deeply thankful to my son Samrat who provided me with photograph to use in the jacket.

Last, but not the least, of M/s Gyan Publishing House, New Delhi, should be specially thanked for his perseverance and persistence, and for allowing me to interpret his word 'urgent' in my own characteristic way.

Sarthak Sengupta

List of Tables

List of Contributors

M.C. Arun. Department of Anthropology, Manipur University, Canchipur, Imphal, Manipur, 795 003.

Rajat Kanti Das. UGC Emeritus Fellow, Department of Anthropology, Vidyasagar University, Midnapore, West Bengal.

Walter Fernandes. North Eastern Social Research Centre, 110, Kharghuli Road, Guwahati, 781004.

Pranami Garg. North Eastern Social Research Centre, 110, Kharghuli Road, Guwahati, 781004.

Lohit Hazarika. Deputy Registrar, K.K. Handique Open University, Guwahati, Assam.

Sekh Rahim Mondal. Centre for Himalayan Studies, University of North Bengal, Raja Rammohanpur, Darjeeling, 734 013, West Bengal.

Rajatsubhra Mukhopadhyay. Department of Sociology, University of North Bengal, Raja Rammohanpur, Darjeeling, 734 013, West Bengal.

S.K. Nanda. Department of Rural Development and Agricultural Production, North-Eastern Hill University, Tura Campus, Tura, West Garo Hills, 794 002, Meghalaya.

Girin Phukan. Department of Political Science, Dibrugarh University, Assam, 786 004.

Rudraman Thapa. Department of Political Science, Dibrugarh University, Dibrugarh, Assam, 786 004.

Lucy Zehol. Department of Anthropology, North-Eastern Hill University, Umshing, Mawkynroh, Shillong Meghalaya, 793 022.

1 Ethnicity: Some Conceptual, Theoretical and Methodological Considerations

Sekh Rahim Mondal

Background

The study of ethnicity has been a major pre-occupation of anthropology, sociology, political science and other branches of social sciences of contemporary times. Ethnicity is not a simple and isolable social phenomenon, rather interrelated to many other complex social issues. Examining and understanding ethnicity requires multiple dimensions as it operates and channelises through various ways and means. The study of ethnicity requires a wide horizon as it is linked with various aspects of social life and its dynamic character. This chapter is an attempt to highlight some conceptual, theoretical and methodological issues those are very much relevant in understanding the process of ethnicity. The chapter is based on review of various incidental literatures and supported by empirical observations of the author in this field of research for about three decades.

II

Identity, Culture and Ethnicity

The concept of ethnicity is very much linked with the issue of identity and also with the aspects of culture. Hence, we may examine ethnicity from the perspective of identity. One way of understanding this phenomenon is to view identity as a collective true self buried beneath layers of superficial and artificial selves. This hidden essential self is one that has deep-rooted historical continuity, shares common codes with others of similar descent, and when discovered and consciously affirmed, translates as one people. Identity is a matter of real as well as that of virtual and imagination. Identity is not an accomplished end point of a people's history, but a constant process of becoming into one. It is never complete, but, is always temporarily positioned within a particular context that needs to be imaginatively and adaptively interpreted.

Identity has been one of the most problematic and contentious fields of research due to its complex and shifting characters. There is little accord on the definition of identity and also about its nature. However, the main concerns are how identities are created, reproduced, transformed and addressed. The main concerns are whether the nation state is threatened by the increasing profusion of politicised identities, or about the role that modernisation and globalisation plays in new identity formation. There is a point of agreement that the contemporary globalisation does seem to create and solidify the threatened identities.

There is a problem in defining identity because of the fact that the term applies at least four different perspectives, viz. (a) how the individuals of a group perceive themselves, (b) how the persons of a group are perceived by others (other groups), (c) how the individuals and group are perceived by the State, and how the persons of a group are perceived by the social scientists and media. For example, the identification of the groups in India as tribes, scheduled tribes, *adivasis,* castes, scheduled castes, *jatis,* OBCs, MOBCs, and minorities are always contested and debated.

It is also to be noted here that the way those people understand themselves, very seldom coincides with the way the others perceive them. Edward (1979) noted that many westerners created stereotypes about the peoples of the Orient which have been adopted by Orientals themselves. It is conspicuously visible that the Indians only identify themselves as Indians when dealing with non-Indians. But among themselves, they are of different groups and they identify other Indians according to their social designations as tribes, castes, linguistic groups, religious groups (recently, as minorities). There is a common tendency of the social scientists to equate tribes as "ethnicities". But it is also true that many tribes also prefer this term, partly because of its common usage and partly because they identify word "tribal" with a proud past and for political rights, and above all, for administrative reasons and protective discrimination.

Self-identity changes from context to context and there are simultaneously overlapping and shifting identities of the same individual or group. Moreover, popular as well as generalised and stereotyped monolithic classification or perception of an individual or group by the other is highly unrealistic and unscientific as it ignores the diversities of identities. Identity is never singular rather highly plural as well as contextual and hence these are to be reflected in the study of ethnicity.

Up to 1950s, the study of identity was not a major issue because the groups that anthropologists studied seemed to be bounded, circumscribed, and obviously delineated by language and culture. If the subject of identity was an issue, it was coined in terms of "national character", "group personality", "patterns of culture", etc., where culture was conceived as a sort of straitjacket identity into which concerned individuals or groups were confined. It was the structure-functionalists who made it easy to take the synchronic view, analysing cultures and identities as they would in case of a still photograph, a slice out of time, unambiguously bounded with well organised structure, but devoid of history and wider context. But the Manchester school under Max Gluckman and others made studies on groups in recognising the fluidity of boundaries, the centrality of conflict by taking the necessity of history and context, especially the changes under colonialism, where people become organised and so-called modernised.

In the context of identity and boundary, the work of Fredrik Barth is quite significant. Barth holds the view that the common culture may not be the primary and definitional characteristic of any social/ethnic group organisation. Rather, he emphasised the fact that culture is nothing but an implication of result of intergroup relations. For Barth, cultural features, that signal the boundary of a cultural/ethnic group, keep constantly changing. He noted that cultural groups use cultural features as signals and emblems of differences while others are ignored, and in some relationships radical differences are played down and denied. He opined that constant interaction among different cultural groups result not only in the formation of common codes and values, but also in structuring of interaction which allows the persistence of cultural differences. Actually, it is not all aspects of a culture making the cultural boundaries, rather the cultural fault lines sharing the boundaries for the sake of identity (Barth, 1969).

However, the study of identity issue did not really matter as of being great concern until the anthropological self-questioning (reflexivity) emerged in the late 1970s and 1980s, when post-modernism shifted attention away from objective structures and facts to the subjective experience of the people being studied and examined. Documenting the voice of the marginal and subalterns, or learning the marginal and alternative discourses, actually gave attention to examine the multiple ways as to the people belong to or not belong to a group and how they identify under such context.

What is very true in the contemporary times is that many elements of traditional cultures of different groups with different identities are very quickly diminishing. There is a direct relationship between population growth, migration, modernisation, demise of language and social change. As a matter of fact, the cultural elements, which once have been the basic marking of identity, are relegated to the background with nothing to do much with identity manifestation. Nowaday's ethnicity is the source of identity on different counts. The multiple processes of globalisation are creating a global arena of potential identity formation reflecting the interaction between locally specific practices of selfhood and the dynamics of global positioning in terms of ethnicity and power. In this context, what is very interesting to note that is, in the globalising world, when many of the traditional cultural elements of the groups or communities are quickly diminishing, why the identities of the different groups or communities are increasing today? This vital question is required to be solved from the nature and characters or ethnicity (Barth, 1969; Hall, 1990; Lewellen, 2002; Rutherford, 1990).

III

Ethnic Group, Ethnicity and Ethno-genesis

For understanding ethnicity, it is very necessary to know about the concept of an 'ethnic group'. An ethnic group is a self-perceived group of people who hold common set of culture and tradition which is not shared by others with whom they are in contact. It denotes a particular group expressed in terms of a sense of continuity in belonging (Vivelo, 1978). Ethnic Group is a social group with a common cultural tradition which exists within a larger society. An ethnic group manages to maintain some distinctive identity that differentiates members of that group from others in the larger society for example—dress, custom, language and so-forth (Burton Wright II et al.,1975).

The term "ethnic" is derived from Greek word "ethnos" meaning heathen, i.e., who is neither of Jews, Christians, Muslims nor Buddhists, or Hindus, or for that matter, of any other religion, but falls under the category of the "Others", i.e., to say, animists or tribes. The noun form "ethnicity" did not appear in the Oxford English Dictionary until 1972, whereas its usage was attributed to sociologist David Reisman in 1953 itself. It is very interesting to note that classical anthropology tended to focus much on ostensibly closed, isolated tribal, peasant and aboriginal or indigenous societies, and by 1950s to 1960s, most of these groups were being structurally absorbed into the larger nation state and many of their individuals were moving, either temporarily or permanently to cities or urban places. As a result, the term "ethnicity" emerged to examine their socio-political dynamics under changed circumstances. Ethnicity came to refer to groups that lived in mutual contact, rather than in isolation, but are clearly different from each other. An "ethnic group", then, becomes a relative concept, dependent on the perception of difference and stigmatised by the notion of "other". Ethnicity merges class distinctions within the ethnic group itself. But the fact is that the ethnic leaders are usually from socio-economically higher category of the same ethnic community. But in terms of depressed class (disadvantaged or marginal), quite different ethnicities may be clubbed together, say, ethnic associations and conglomerations. Ethnicity is often relative to a particular territory, usually a country or region. Thus, it appears that in recent times, the term ethnic group or ethnicity has a wider implication not restricted to so-called tribal or indigenous communities.

Nowadays, the term ethnicity is even used to identify the non-tribal groups living in multi-cultural societies, particularly the migrants mostly confined to ghettos or certain parts of the country where boundaries are largely social based upon perceived differences. For example, the Asians living in USA and UK and many other non-Asian countries. But in social science research, the term ethnicity is still more used to denote marginal, disadvantaged, excluded and minority communities who are confronting with the dominant majorities. Ethnicity is basically an issue of "ours" and "others". Actually, imaging "other" and "otherness" is the root of ethnic differentiation.

In fact, it is very difficult to define ethnicity; if it can be defined at all, it should be conceived as a selfconscious and projected group identity that emphasises and naturalises one or usually a number of specific attributes, such as skin colour, language, religion, place of origin, ancestry, descent or territory (Tamtriah, 1996). Ethnicity is self-conscious and/or projected identity because it refers to a self-defined group with some sort of collective identity say for example Bodo, Adivasi, Gorkha, and Deshi, and so on. Ethnicity is a matter of degree on two counts. It is the degree to which the people themselves have a sense of common identity and it is also the degree to which surrounding peoples/groups perceive them to be different. Hence, the perception of we/ours and they/others actually dictates the idea of ethnicity. Ethnic identification is also situational to a certain extent say- an Indian citizen may be an Indian first and an inhabitant like, Assomia, Bangali, and Oriya, etc., last while being an Indian one and the same time.

Ethnicity is usually perceived as the strategy of interest alliance. The nature of exposition of ethnicity under the circumstance depends to a major extent on the kind of stimulus received by an individual or a group at a given point of time.

Ethnicity presupposes multiplicity of identities and inherent plural loyalties on social, political, cultural and other counts. Importance of boundary in the understanding of the problems of ethnicity is considered very crucial. Ethnicity from the perspective of border manifests the apparent clash of cultural and political mechanisms of boundary maintenance. Ethnicity is considered as a process, whereby the leaders of an ethnic group try to mobilise its group members by utilising the ethnic sentiment for some economic and political goals (Danda, 1991).

The most crucial aspect of examining ethnicity is the relationship between majority and minority groups. It is an awkward question to raise that, do majority and dominant group(s) comprise as "ethnic"? Or do they have "ethnicity"? It is a highly complex question in anthropology and other social sciences. Ethnicity represents a relation of power, and as a result, a group is 'ethnic' only within the wider socio-political field. Since dominant or majority group(s) control everything, as such, it has the power to define who is 'ethnic' and who is not as it never considers itself as 'ethnic'. Similarly, whoever controls the dominant discourse determines as to who gets named "ethnic" and who does not. Since the dominant group considers itself as an universal or essential group, and thereby the referent culture for all others, as such, it is above ethnicity (Wilmsen, 1996; Foucault, 1988).

For examining ethnicity, it is necessary to know the dynamics or process of becoming 'ethnic'. Ethnicity is linked with 'ethno-genesis' which is nothing but the process by which people become ethnic minded. Usually, it involves both the wider society and the people themselves. Prejudice, stigmatisation, exclusion, and rejection of a group may create a feeling of marginality and self-consciousness that stimulates individuals of a group to reflect on forgotten histories and unconscious cultural elements, and thereby, organise around them. The actual practice of ethnicity is determined by relative position of a group in power hierarchy at local and wider context. From this perspective, ethnic politics is also called as politics of division and marginalisation or politics of culture.

The emergence of ethnicity may be seen as a part of modernisation/ globalisation process. In multiethnic and multicultural countries, ethnicity is entirely a matter of forced assimilation, exclusion, and ghettoisation. In this context, ethnicity to some extent is a conscious individual/self-decision. Hence, it is an aspect of a community or a group identity and it is the situations and circumstances that make ethnicisation appealing. It is quite easier to view ethnicity largely in terms of culture, but real understanding of ethnicity require a broad vision of interrelationship in relation to resources utilisation and position in power structure. A number of global forces are now converging to generate the present wave of ethnic politics. Ethnicity and ethnic politics may be called as politics of presence.

In the globalised era, the forces of cultural homogenisation have caused gradual loss of identities and diversities thereby leading to a counter effect making the heterogeneous subaltern groups more identity-conscious in the process through ethno-cultural lines at the local context (Cohen, 1978; Danda, 1991; Tambiah, 1996; Lewellen, 2002; Phukon, 2002).

IV

Theorising Ethnicity and Ethnic Theories

The subject of ethnicity has to be studied from different theoretical perspectives. Primordialism, constructionism and Relationalism are very central to theorising ethnicity. There has always been a debate between primordialists and constructionists with regard to theorising ethnicity.

Primordialism is the idea that the ethnicity is based on some deeply inscribed long-term group cohesion with manifest claims to blood, soil, language, and mythologised history. From the viewpoint of primordialism, skin colour, hair, height and other physical features are taken into account for group cohesion and identification. The implication is that the ethnic groups have been genetically inbred population in which culture has become conjoined. But it is to be admitted that culture has less relation with biology and each culture has its own history and own process of environmental adaptation. Thus, defining ethnicity in terms of biological and cultural attributes is highly inappropriate. According to primordialists, ethnicity is a primal condition, such as a tribe or a group into which one is born. It is a form of essentialism, in the sense that it involves an ongoing relatively unchanging group identity. For various reasons, under changing context, primordialism is no longer considered much valid to examine the contemporary process of ethnicity. Primordialism has now been conjoined to instrumentalism, which means, weakened or threatened tribal or ethnic solidarity has been reinforced by some sort of group utility, such as, control over trade routes, access to valued resources, maintenance of territory by autonomy, or a political need to present a united front against governmental infringements. As per instrumentalist view, ethnicity emerges when some sort of collective identity would benefit them materially such as maintaining ownership of territory, or controlling a particular resource of their territory. This is also regarded as neo-primordialism. Western anthropology has a tradition to relate ethnicity to tribalism, viewing tribal groups moving to cities and retaining the cultural characteristics of rural identities. In former Soviet Union, an extreme form of primordialism is used to analyse by making use of ethnos theory.

On the other hand, constructionism views ethnicity not as simply the survival/revival of ancient tribalism, but as collective identity construction (formation) either by group itself or by the dominant group. It considers ethnicity to be the result of collective action of both the tribal minority as well as the dominant (cultural) majority. It is very important to note that the way ethnic people understand themselves very seldom coincides with the way the others perceive them. Constructionism is regarded as the most dominant theoretical perspective in examining the subject of ethnicity. It states that ethnicity is always constructed situationally and is in constant flux, and thus, flatly rejects primordialism. Constructionism may be categorised into two sub types, viz., cultural constructionism and political constructionism. Cultural constructionism advocates that where a group constructs its identity through shared symbols and practices, these have traditionally been called culture. Here, the shared cultural elements are ingredients in formulation of group cohesion and reproduction. The cultural belongings give a sense of meaning to community identity. While in political constuctionism, the elites (tribes or ethnic) within the nation state, fashion a dominant set of ideologies, artistic styles, and linguistic usages which become normative under such situations. Ethnicities are created by exclusion and marginalisation. In this context, groups are built up out of a cost benefit analysis, in which some sort of objective interests or common goals, such as maintaining control of an economic niche, is the prime motive for group formation.

The relationalism rejects both primordialist and constructionalist interpretation of identity formation and ethnicity of a group. Relationalism indicates that treating ethnicity as a noun that refers to a bounded set of groups, makes no sense as, in changing context, no specific characteristic or group of characteristics are common to all the members, even within the same group. Thus, it regards that ethnicity must refer to relationship between the groups. Actually, identities are not "things" but relational ethnicity has its historical origins in inequality. It manifests in the activities of daily life, especially in encounters between the ethnic group and the dominant power in a nation. Once established, ethnicity takes on a powerful feeling tone, so that the groups seem primaordial which will then be mystified.

In addition to above theoretical perspectives, radical historicism is also getting popularity in ethnic theories. This is basically a Marxist approach in which social identities are created historically over long periods out of division of labour, class struggle, and class consciousness focused on material condition and mode of production (Banks, 1996; Comaroff, 1996; Cohen, 1969; Erikson, 1993; Lewellen, 2002; Wilmsen, 1996).

V

Epilogue

The study of ethnicity requires conceptual clarity, appropriate theoretical perspective and sound methodology. Identity, inequality, marginality and power hierarchy are very much linked with the issue of ethnicity. Hence, the ethnic problem is to be examined holistically and analytically. The term 'tribe', 'ethnic group', 'ethnic minority' has been now gradually replaced by the phrase 'indigenous community' which has come in forefront in examining the process of ethnicity. Thus, the nexus between 'ethnicity' and 'indigenousity' requires to be examined critically in the empirical context. The understanding of ethnicity also requires a gender perspective. The way of revival of some traditional cultural elements of an ethnic group is also an important area of enquiry. The politicisation of culture is one of the major dimensions of ethnicity and which is very much genderised in nature. It is to be borne in mind that ethnicity is not only the result of frustration but also is a mechanism of generating hopes and aspirations amongst the members of the concerned group.

Ethnicity is the outcome of globalisation process. Numbers of global forces are now converging to generate the present wave of ethnicity. How the local ethnic issues are linked to the global ethnic movements, or vice-versa, is a new area of enquiry. Tribal or ethnic-political mobilisation has been increasing day by day through the recognition of 'indigenous rights' by official organisations like UNO and Non-Governmental Institutions. These have serious impacts on the life of the tribal, both at the local, and also at the global levels.

The tribals, particularly the tribal or ethnic leaders, are now aware about their rights to preserve customs and cultures, the right of self-governance, maintenance of traditional economic activities and language, protection of indigenous environment and indigenous representation in governing bodies. The United Nations Declaration of 1993 as the Year of Indigenous People and period 1995-2005 as the Decade of Indigenous People has helped in legitimising tribal resistance. All these have direct or indirect linkages with the ethnic processes which need to be enquired thoroughly.

Usually, ethnicity has been looked upon from negative angle; therefore, the issue of ethnicity was mostly tagged with social unrest.

But this is not always true. Ethnicity has some positive aspects too as it helps in maintaining and conserving the valuable cultural resources, of which, the most important is indigenous knowledge (IK) or traditional knowledge (TK) or indigenous wisdom (IW).

There has been a tendency among the scholars of 'other' culture to examine the issue of ethnicity from their own (etic) perspective; considered thus, it is a social or political problem. But, post-modernism shifted our attention away from supposedly objective structures and facts to the subjective experience of the people being studied. Rendering a voice to subalterns and learning of marginal discourses are nowadays very important in social scientific research. Thus, the understanding of ethnicity also requires an interpretative and people's (etic) perspective. In the study of ethnicity, the relation and position between researcher and researched seems to be very important as because it is the issue of "ethnogenesis" on the part of researcher (outsider), but "ethnic assertion" or "self assertion" on the part of the researched.

Ethnicity may be examined from varied angles. It may be viewed from the structural, attributional, and interactional point of views. From social-structural angle, ethnicity is about social and cultural differentiation which has reference to identity projection. From attributional point of view, ethnicity is a process in which "ethnic awareness" and "ethnic consciousness" plays the most vital role. Whereas, from interactional point of view, ethnicity is the outcome of relations and interactions between "we" and "they" or "self" and "others" in the day to day social affairs. Ethnicity is subjective experience and belief of a particular group but manifests through several objective criteria.

References

Banks, Marcus. 1996. *Ethnicity: Ethnological Constructions,* New York: Rutledge.

Barth, Frederik. 1969. *Ethnic Groups and Boundaries: The Social Organisation of Culture Difference,* London: George Allen and Unwin.

Burton Wright II; John P. Weiss and Charles M. Unkovic. 1975. *Perspective: An Introduction to Sociology,* Illinois: The Dryden Press.

Cohen, Abner. 1969, *Custom and Politics in Urban Africa: A Study of Hansa Migrants in a Yoruba Towa,* Barkley: University of California Press.

Cohen, Ronald. 1978. 'Ethnicity: Problem and focus in anthropology', *Annual Review of Anthropology,* 7: 379-403.

Comaroff. John L. 1996. 'Ethnicity, nationalism and the politics of difference in the age of revolution'. In E.M. Wilmsen and P. McAllisen (Eds.): *The Politics of Difference: Ethnic Premises in a World of Power,* Chicago: Chicago University Press.

Danda, A.K. 1991. *Ethnicity in India,* New Delhi: Inter India Publications.

Erikson Thomas Hyland. 1998. *Ethnicity and Nationalism: Anthropological Perspectives,* London: Pluto Press.

Foucault, Michel. 1988. *Madness and Civilization,* Translated by Richard Howard, New York : Vintage.

Hall, Stuart. 1990. 'Cultural Identity and Diaspora'. In J. Rutherford (Ed.): *Identity, Community, Culture, Difference,* London: Lawrence and Wishart.

Lewellen, Ted C. 2002. *The Anthropology of Globalisation,* London: Bergin and Garvey.

Phukon, Girin. 2002, *Ethnicity and Polity in South Asia,* New Delhi: South Asian Publishing Pvt. Ltd.

Rutherford, J. 1990. *Identity, Community, Culture, Difference,* London: Lawrence and Wishart.

Tambiah, Stanley J. 1996. 'The Nation State in Crisis and the Rise of Ethnonationalism'. In E.N. Wilemsen and P. McAllister (Eds.): *The Politics of Difference: Ethnic Premises in a World of Power,* Chicago: University of Chicago Press.

Vivelo, Frank Robert. 1978. *Cultural Anthropology Hand Book,* New York: McGrant Hill Book Company.

Wilmsen, Edwin, E.N. and P. McAllister. 1996. *The Politics of Difference: Ethnic Premises in a World of Power,* Chicago: University of Chicago Press.

2 Ethnicity and Nation-building in India: A Critical Appreciation with Special Reference to North East India

S.K. Nanda

Ethnicity and nation-building have been discussed for quite some time now. It is usually believed that ethnicity, especially in multicultural or multinational countries, poses serious challenges and threats to the process of nation-building. It is also argued that assertion of ethnic identity is detrimental and antithetical to the unity and integrity of a multicultural country. This sort of reasoning, both in academic discourse and common parlance, seems to have originated from an erroneous conceptualisation of ethnicity or ethnic identity, on the one hand, and a very restricted and conventional understanding of nation-building, on the other. The erroneous conceptualisation of ethnicity and the conventional understanding of nation-building not only confuses ethnic group with cultural nation (i.e. nation in cultural sense) but also blurs the distinction between nation and state as well as ethnicity and regional nationalism in multicultural or multinational countries. As a result, serious misconception and misunderstanding about the process of nation-building in such countries perpetuate in different parts of the world. It is, thus, essential to understand ethnicity and nation-building in their proper perspectives to have an appropriate process of the latter in multicultural context. This chapter proposes to examine ethnicity and nation-building in their proper perspectives in the multicultural context of India with special reference to the North Eastern region so that the ambiguities surrounding these terms can be hopefully dispelled and an appropriate strategy of nation-building be developed for countries like India.

Ethnicity and Nation-building: A Conceptual Note

Ethnicity is one of the most elusive concepts in social science vocabulary. This is so because, ethnicity has been mostly interpreted loosely, and keeping the sovereignty (or state-centric) aspect in the understanding of nation in view, scholars tend to dub all the cultural communities—big or small, in majority or in minority, natives or outsiders—of a multicultural state as ethnic groups or ethnicities and their respective cultural identities as ethnic identities. In other words, the entire population of a multicultural state is referred to as a nation and the constituent cultural communities of this population are labeled as ethnic groups. However, the fact of the matter is that most of these cultural communities constitute distinct nations in cultural sense of the term, and hence, cannot be adjudged as ethnic groups.

It may be noted that the term 'ethnic group', derived etymologically from the Greek word 'ethnos', originally meant a race or a primitive culture or autochthonous group or a tribe or a nation (Cashmore, 1984; Glazer and Moynihan, 1975; Isaac, 1975). Derived from the Italian word *'natio'* or the French word *'nascion'*, nation also originally meant race or cultural community or ethnic group (Hayes, 2006; Lesley, 1993). This means that in their original conception, both ethnic group and nation were understood in cultural sense and they meant almost the same thing. But in modern times (i.e. from the last quarter of 17th century) as sovereign states were constituted on national lines, or as nations organised themselves into independent states, the term nation came to be increasingly interpreted in sovereign sense and the meaning of nation as a sovereign political unit gained preponderance. However, a closer examination reveals that, historically, the emergence of nation as a sovereign political entity was based on two conceptions: political and cultural (Smith, 1986). The political conception emphasised the civil-political characteristics of nation such as popular sovereignty, common citizenship, common legal-administrative system, defined geo-political boundary, etc. The cultural conception, on the contrary, highlighted common language, common culture, shared history, common descent, and common ancestral or adopted territory as the chief characteristics of nation.

Based on the civil-political conception, Britain, France, Holland, Spain and the U.S.A. emerged as sovereign nations, whereas, following the cultural conception, Germany, Italy, Greece, Poland and the Balkan countries were organised as independent nations. In either case, however, nation is viewed in sovereign sense. While, in most Asian and African countries, especially the former colonies, the political and cultural conceptions of nation unfolded simultaneously, though at different levels. At the macro-political or overarching state level, the political notion emerged, and in this context, nation invariably meant an organised sovereign political grouping of people; but, at the micro or regional level; nation was viewed as a distinct cultural unit and the sovereignty element was not considered as essential for its existence. This dual conception of nation and nationalism existed in most of the ex-colonial countries during the colonial period and it continues to exist in these countries in post-colonial times as well (Geertz, 1971; Desai, 1966). The preponderance of multicultural or multinational States the world over, reinforce the political and cultural notion of nation further.

It is thus evident from the experience of several countries that nation can be conceptualised in both political and cultural terms. In political sense, nation invariably means a sovereign unit, but in cultural sense, nation does not necessarily mean a sovereign entity. Sovereignty is an essential feature for a State, and not for a nation, to exist. A State, by definition and implication, is a sovereign political unit and it has the monopoly of authority over its sovereign territory. Without sovereignty, a State cannot exist; but a nation can exist without sovereignty. A nation may have its own State, or form a part of a State, or split up into two or more States, or exist without any political structure of its own (Nanda, 2007).

However, the fact of the matter is that, nation in cultural sense, resembles ethnic group. Hence, the question is how ethnic group can be distinguished from nation in cultural sense. It is true that nation and ethnic group share many socio-cultural attributes in common, but they differ in respect of one crucial variable, i.e., the possession of homeland—ancestral or adopted. In cultural sense, nation means a cultural community with ancestral or adopted homeland and having the potential for being politically organised into a self-ruling and self-sustaining unit. To quote Oommen (1996: 32), "a nation does not come into being unless it establishes a legitimate claim over a territory which in turn provides it with the potential to state formation". However, an ethnic group connotes a people who share a common culture but do not inhabit in their ancestral or traditional homeland. This means that ethnics are people who belong to alien cultures but are placed in the territory of another people due to dislocation from their home territory. In modern times, several factors such as colonisation, conquest and above all migration gave rise to this dislocation. In this context, Weber very rightly observed that an ethnic group refers to "those human groups that entertain a subjective belief in their common descent because of similarities in physical type or of customs or of both, or because of memories of colonisation and migration" (Weber, 1978: 389). Smith noted that ethnic group or ethnicity is a group of people whose members identify with each other usually based on a presumed common genealogy or ancestry (Smith, 1986). Oommen (1990: 10) also noted that an ethnic group is "a group of people who share a common history, culture, language and life style but are uprooted from or unattached to a homeland". Barth (1969) observes that ethnic groups are boundary-maintaining groups that result from subjective process of status identification. To Cohen (2004), ethnicity is more of an urban phenomenon. Jenkins (1997), however, considers ethnic groups as power groups or pressure groups. According to him, ethnic identifications are constructed as social formations because of power relations. Eriksen (2002) argues that far from being an immutable property, ethnicity is a dynamic and shifting aspect of relationship. This means that ethnic group is mostly defined in a specific sense to mean distinct cultural groups in the midst of a larger community.

It is thus clear that, homeland and not political sovereignty, is the crucial variable that distinguishes a nation from an ethnic group in cultural sense. The chief attributes of an ethnic group are shared culture and a sense of group distinctiveness; whereas the chief elements of nation in cultural sense are common culture, a geographically contiguous ancestral or adopted home territory and potentiality for self-determination. For conceptual clarity, nation in cultural sense can be referred to as 'cultural nation'. Viewed in this sense, the people living in their homelands and having the potential for self-determination can be termed as cultural nations and not ethnic groups. To cite an example, the English in England, the Russians in Russia, the Bengalis in West Bengal, the Tamils in Tamil Nadu, the Assamese in Assam, etc., are cultural nations and not ethnic groups. However, taking the criteria of cultural difference and group distinctiveness into consideration, scholars tend to consider all types of cultural communities, including the ones possessing homelands and the potentiality for self-rule, as ethnic groups (Phadnis, 1990). Going by this logic, the English in England, the Scotts in Scotland, the Russians in Russia, the Bengali in West Bengal, etc., are referred to as ethnic groups.

Both cultural nation and ethnic group can be politically mobilised. When an ethnic group becomes politically mobile, it calls for protectionist treatment, or it may evolve into a nation by securing a homeland. However, in the case of cultural nation, political mobilisation may lead to demand for self-rule in autonomous (i.e. council or provincial unit) or sovereign terms. The ethnification of a cultural nation is also possible and this happens only when it is marginalised and loses its claim over its own territory, or is apportioned among several political units (e.g. the Kurds in West Asia, the Tripuris in Tripura, etc.).

It follows from the above discussion that ethnic groups are different from cultural nations and that the multicultural States all over the world contain both ethnic groups and cultural nations. Ethnic groups in these states mainly include; (a) dispersed or scattered cultural minorities (linguistic or religious groups) who have no territory of their own but identify with common territory of the State or the country of their location; (b) immigrants and foreigners; (c) peripheral and marginal groups; (d) displaced people and outsiders; and (e) very small number of indigenous people or smaller tribal groups with a home territory but not able to be organised as self-sustaining units.

The concept of nation is central to the process of nation-building. However, there cannot be only one form of nation-building throughout the world. In other words, nation- building should not be viewed in a conventional way only. Nation-building efforts may vary from place to place. In conventional sense, nation-building simply means creating national unity among the people of a State through common cultural bonds. At a deeper level, it refers to the process of constructing or structuring a nation using the State power. This process aims at unification or homogenisation of the people within the State so that it remains politically united and viable in the long run. The process includes the creation of overarching national paraphernalia such as national flag, national anthem, national days, national language, national history and myths, common political institutions, etc. It also involves the use of propaganda and major infrastructure development to foster social integration and economic growth.

The process of nation-building is as old as the origin of nations in modern sense. As already mentioned, in some parts of Europe and America, nations emerged following the civil-political model; and in some other parts of Europe, nations were formed using the linguistic-cultural model. In the former case, the efforts of nation-building were directed at homogenising the people by constructing a uniform cultural base and this was done by adopting a common language as the main instrument of cultural homogeneity, e.g., English in U.K. and U.S.A., French in France, Spanish in Spain, Dutch in Netherlands, etc. But in the latter case, nation-building efforts aimed at creating common civil-political basis for a culturally homogeneous people, e.g., the Germans, Italians, Greeks, Hungarians, etc. However, in either case, the nation-state formula and cultural homogeneity were identified as the benchmark of conventional nation-building. But the application of the conventional model of nation-building in several Asian and African countries led to disastrous and dangerous consequences for national unity. As mentioned earlier, in these countries nation assumes a civil-political connotation at the macro or state level, and a cultural connotation at the micro or regional-cultural level. Adoption of conventional nation-building in terms of the nation-state formula and cultural homogeneity in such countries means homogenisation and assimilation of the culturally diverse people in terms of culture, language and religion of the mainstream nation or majority community. This, in turn, results in destruction or suppression of regional cultural nationalities and ethnic diversities (Connor, 1973). Regional-cultural nations and ethnic groups in multicultural states therefore, resist the conventional nation-building model strongly. In their perception, nation-building is not nation-breaking or withering away of ethnic diversities.

Judging from this viewpoint, nation-building process in multicultural countries should be based on the multicultural or multinational perspective and not on the nation-state model or the cultural framework of majority/mainstream community. The multicultural perspective of nation-building in such countries should focus on the dual conception of nation: (a) civil-political content of nation at the macro-political level and (b) cultural content of nation at the regional level. In other words, nation building in this context should focus on the civil framework of the State at the macro level and the cultural framework of the people at the micro level. In multicultural countries, the concept of nationhood at the macro level should not be identified with any individual nation/nationality or category of people; it should be associated with the plurality of the people and should reflect the civil-political conception of nation (Parekh, 2000: 341; Ganguly and Macduff, 2003). In these countries, nation-building should aim at constructing national identity at the macro level in political sense and not in cultural sense; the political sense of nation-building views the culturally diverse people as a whole constituting the nation in civil terms. Such an understanding of nation building embodies accommodation of plurality of cultural nationalities and ethnic groups within the common fold of the civic nation. Against this conceptual backdrop, the analysis of ethnicity and nation-building in India in general and North-eastern region in particular, has been done in the following pages.

Ethnicity and Nation-building in India

It is well known that India is a multicultural country with an age-old civilisation spanning over 5000 years. People belonging to different cultural, racial, linguistic, religious and tribal backgrounds came to India at different times and settled down in different parts of her soil thousands of years ago. This apart, several primitive or autochthonous communities, and aboriginal or indigenous people inhabit in different parts of India since time immemorial. In course of time, most of these culturally different people identified themselves with certain geographically contiguous areas within the country and morally claimed those areas as their homelands or native lands. In this way, these peoples developed territorial identity and thereby evolved into distinct nations in cultural sense.

In the modern period, which was marked by British colonial rule in India, some people became mobile and started living outside their traditional homelands because of the socio-economic opportunities unleashed by the modern forces. Some people were also dislodged or uprooted from their traditional lands due to dismemberment of their nationalities by the provincial arrangement of the colonial administration. Further, the colonial rulers transported large number of people from one area to another to work as labourers, subordinate staff and workers in plants and factories. Besides this, the partition of colonial India in 1947 led to huge influx of refugees and migrants from Pakistan to the post-colonial Indian State. Partition also reduced many people into cultural minorities. The integration of 562 Indian princely States with the post-colonial Indian State in 1947-49 further brought in its wake several distinct cultural nationalities and ethnic minorities. The process of cultural and ethnic pluralism is further escalated by the constitution of the liberal democratic State of India which guarantees the right to freedom of movement and residence within the country. The ongoing pace of modernisation and economic development introduced by the independent Indian State also facilitated cross-cultural migration of people within India. In nutshell, the impact of colonisation, partition and subsequent integration of the then-existing States and the liberal political system of free Indian State contribute immensely to the formation of ethnic groups all over India. Along with the cultural nationalities, these ethnic groups added to the stupendous cultural diversity in India.

Thus, the Indian State that emerged following the partition and subsequent integration of native States contains within its fold various cultural nations and numerous ethnic groups. The nation-building approach in the Indian State hence, should primarily focus on integrating these multifarious cultural nations and ethnic groups to create a united or one Indian national identity. But unfortunately, the nation-building process adopted in India followed the nation-state perspective and cultural homogeneity in terms of the majority community. This approach emphasises the concept of Indian nation in cultural sense based on the majority community's language or religion, i.e., Hindi language or Hindu religion. However, this approach has been strongly opposed by several cultural nations and ethnic groups in different parts of India, especially in Jammu and Kashmir, Punjab, Southern, Eastern and North-Eastern region.

It may be noted that as a unified country, India exists in geographic sense since time immemorial. But as a unified cultural unit, India neither existed in the past nor does it exist even now. In addition, as one political unit under a single authority, India emerged only during the colonial period, although attempts at political unity were made in pre-colonial times. But even in the colonial days, there was no common administration in the whole of India; 'British India' was ruled directly and 'Princely India' was ruled by the native princes. Nevertheless, the idea of one India in the colonial period paved the emergence of nationalism in India. However, interestingly, two forms of nationalism emerged at the all-India level: one was anchored to secular-political ideology and the other was grounded in religious ideologies advocated by the Muslim and Hindu religious nationalists. The former adhered to the civil-political conception of nation based on common citizenship, civil rights, common legal administrative system and psychological unity; while the latter stressed the cultural conception of nation in terms of the Muslim and Hindu religion. To this, was added a third variety of nationalism, which largely called for self-rule for cultural nations within the political space of a province. The religious nationalisms, however, finally led to the partition of colonial India and the birth of the independent States of India and Pakistan. As already noted, after independence, numerous native States were merged with the Indian State and with that, one political India in real sense has emerged.

After the establishment of the sovereign Indian State, nationalism at the all-India level remains as a consciousness and it calls for allegiance of the people to the Indian nation. However, the people in India, at large, are not prepared to show allegiance to Indian nation at the cost of their respective cultural nations. In their view the Indian nation exists in civil political sense and their own nations exist in cultural sense and hence, they largely want to identify with two circles/layers of national identity—the pan-Indian and their respective cultural national identities. This dual expression of nationalism has been seen in the growth of regional nationalism demanding provincial States in various parts of independent India (Guha, 1983). The Indian political leadership accepted most of the popular demands and granted provincial statehood to several cultural nationalities and in the process, as many as 28 provinces have been created within the Indian Union from 1947 to 2008. However, the demands by several cultural nations for more provinces persist.

The prevalence of the dual notion of nationality in popular minds and the demands for more provinces prove beyond doubt that the nation-state or mainstream perspective of nation-building cannot be applied to India. The multicultural or multinational perspective acknowledging the dual notion of nationality—pan-Indian, based on common political identity, and regional, based on cultural identity—is the most appropriate model of nation-building for India. It is important to note that the Constitution of India has officially acknowledged and legitimised the multicultural perspective of nation-building in India. The Preamble of the Indian Constitution clearly states that India is a sovereign socialist secular democratic republic State. In fact, it envisages the concept of one-India in plural and not in singular cultural sense. This means that the people of India together with their respective cultural and ethnic identities constitute the Indian nation and that no particular cultural nation or ethnic group in India can be identified with the Indian nationhood.

Further, some fundamental rights of the Indian Constitution such as the right to equality and liberty (Art. 14-18) and right to freedom (Art.19) not only ensure cultural pluralism but also make it obligatory on the part of the State to protect and promote cultural pluralism. Similarly, the right to freedom of religion (Art. 25), the right to preservation of language and script by distinct cultural communities (Art. 29), and the right to run educational institutions by linguistic and religious minorities (Art. 30) strengthen the official recognition of linguistic and religious pluralism. Apart from this, the declaration of Hindi as the official language of the Union under Art. 343 (1), and the recognition of 22 regional languages, including Hindi, in the Eighth Schedule under Art. 344 (1) and 351 certify clearly the Constitutional sanction to the multilingual and multicultural character of Indian nation. The constitution of the official language commission comprising members of the regional languages and the power given to the State governments to declare a regional language as the official or second language of the States reinforce this position further.

It may be noted that the 1971 census of India reported 1,652 languages or mother tongues in India (Nigam, 1971). However, based on numerical strength criterion (i.e. 10,000 and above speakers), the 1991 census of India listed 114 distinct languages or mother tongues in India. Out of this, 22 are scheduled languages and the remaining languages belong to non-scheduled category. The Constitution of India originally listed 14 Indian languages in the Eighth Schedule, but under popular pressure, Sindhi (in 1967), Konkani, Manipuri and Nepali (in 1992), Bodo, Dogri, Maithili and Santhali (in 2003) were declared as scheduled languages. Notwithstanding this, Hindi has been often claimed by official effort and by North Indian perception as the only national language. It is also claimed that Indian nationhood, in cultural sense, should be identified with Hindi alone and that the nation-building efforts in India should recognise Hindi as the common language for construction of Indian national identity. It is true that Hindi-speakers constitute nearly 40.27 per cent of the Indian population (Census of India, 1991); but that does not mean Hindi is the common language in India. Out of 28 States and six union territories, Hindi language is spoken in nine States and the national capital city of Delhi. In the rest of the 19 States and five union territories, the other scheduled languages and numerous non-scheduled languages are spoken. Out of the 22 scheduled languages, 12 languages have more than 10 million speakers and each one of them is identified with a particular Indian State. Besides, most of the scheduled languages are declared as the official languages of several States. Not only that, most of the scheduled languages are even older to Hindi and some of them have stronger literary tradition than Hindi.

Again, the official claim that Hindi is the most widely spoken language in India does not match with the ground reality in the so-called Hindi belt (Brass, 1974). Under the official rubric of Hindi language, several distinct mother tongues, such as Bhojpuri, Awadhi, Brij bhasa, Khari boli, Bundelkhandi, Haryanavi, Pahari, Kumaoni, Gharwali, Marwari, etc., are spoken in their respective ancestral lands. If these languages are officially acknowledged, the percentage of Hindi will be much lower than what is projected. It may further be noted that Maithili was officially recorded under Hindi until it was accorded scheduled status in 2003. In some of the Hindi States also, Urdu is recognised as the second official language. Hence, the claim that Hindi is 'the national language' or 'the common language' of India nation is incorrect. Indian nationhood is multilingual in character and it cannot be identified with a particular language only.

However, the protagonists of the mainstream perspective of nation-building made significant efforts from time to time to articulate Indian nationhood in terms of Hindi only. For example, during the period of single-partydominance in Indian politics from 1947 to 1996, the central political leadership represented mainly by the Congress party tried to promote nation-building through Hindi language. In 1965, it was decided to switch over to Hindi as the only official language of the Union and drop English as the associate official language after its completion of 15-year term from the commencement of the Constitution in 1950. However, as vehement opposition was raised in the non-Hindi speaking Southern and Eastern Indian States, the decision was revoked and English was allowed to continue as the associate language beyond the 15-year term. Thereafter, the three-language formula was adopted to popularise the case of Hindi as the common Indian language. However, this experiment did not gain grounds in the Southern Indian provinces. The Constitution of India empowers the Union to promote Hindi as a language of communication and expression, but most of the Indian people are not ready to embrace Hindi at the cost of their own language and identity. In fact, people in India, largely, are ready to accept Hindi and English as the official languages of the Union as well as the link languages in practically the whole of India. It is important to note that the recognition of 22 scheduled languages and the acceptance of these languages as the medium of instruction and as literary subjects in schools and colleges very strongly establish the plural linguistic identity of India and hence any attempt of nation-building implying forceful 'Hindiisation' of Indian nationhood will meet with crisis.

The advocates of the mainstream perspective of nation-building not only emphasise Hindi language but also the vociferous adherents of this perspective, comprising the Rastriya Swayam Sevak Sangh (RSS), Bharatiya Janata Party (BJP), Vishwa Hindu Parishad (VHP) and their ally, the Shiv Sena, constantly articulate Indian nationhood in terms of Hindu religion. Their ideology is simply based on the view that the majority of Indians are Hindus and therefore, Hinduism should provide the cultural basis of Indian nationhood. The Hindus constitute 80.5 per cent of Indian population (Census of India, 2001). However, the attempt to identify Indian nation with Hindus only would mean denial of right to nationality, power, privilege and prestige to 200 million (20 per cent) Indian people comprising the minority religious groups such as the Muslims (13 per cent), Christians (2 per cent), Sikhs (1.2 per cent), etc. (Census of India, 2001). It may be noted that as many as nine major religions—five religions of foreign origin, such as, Islam, Christianity, Zoroastrianism, Judaism and Bahai' Faith and four religions of Indian origin, such as, Hinduism, Buddhism, Jainism and Sikhism—and scores of indigenous and tribal religions exist in India. The conception of Indian nationhood in terms of Hinduism only, which is popularly called as '*Hindutva*' or '*Hindu Rastravad*', would also mean forceful absorption or exclusion of minority religions. The identification of Indian nation solely with the Hindus also negates the secular fabric of the Indian Constitution.

Furthermore, the logic that Hinduism provides a source of cultural unity in India seems baseless. Not only Hindus lack horizontal unity, but also, there is no vertical unity among them as they are hierarchically divided into 250 castes and sub-castes arranged within the fold of the four major caste divisions (*varnas*): Brahmins, Kshatriyas, Vaishyas and Sudras. The caste factor divides the Hindus more than it unites them. The three major caste segments of Hindu community—the upper castes, the other backward castes (OBCs) and the scheduled castes (Dalits)—compete against each other for political supremacy and social domination (Khan, 1987). Politically, the Dalits align more with the backward Muslims, and along with the OBCs and the Muslims, the Dalits want to capture political power. However, the political ascendancy of the Dalits and the OBCs is not acceptable to the upper castes—the so-called custodian of Hindu religion and the champions of Hindu Indian nation.

Hindus are also divided along regional lines: North India is associated with Aryan Hindus and South India with Dravidian Hindus. The Aryan dominated North India flaunts a sense of supremacy over the Dravidian dominated South India. Linguistic divisions also impair Hindu unity. Hindus are divided into numerous linguistic nationalities and the practice of Hinduism differs from one nationality to another. In addition, the linguistic nationalities in India contain people from diverse religious faiths. Hence, the identification of Indian nation with the Hindus would break these nationalities along religious lines. Last but not the least, the religions of Hindu origin such as Sikhism, Buddhism and Jainism resent their inclusion under the category of

Hinduism in the Constitution of India. Some Sikhs responded to the Hindu claim in a militant manner. This means that a monolithic Hindu identity does not exist in India; Hindu society is plural and owing to its internal divisions, it cannot provide a unified cultural basis to Indian nation. India is a multi-religious country, and therefore, Indian nationhood cannot be associated with the majority Hindu religion only. Thus, looking at the empirical situation of India, it can be certainly argued that the articulation of Indian nationhood from mainstream perspective, i.e., the Hindi language or the Hindu religion, will not be practically feasible or tenable. In fact, any nation-building effort that considers India as a nation in the cultural sense is grossly erroneous because India cannot and should not be conceptualised as a nation in the cultural sense. India is a nation in civil-political sense with plural cultural base (Khan, 1994; Vijapur, 1998); the Indian people belonging to several cultural nations, and ethnic groups together constitute the Indian nation.

Ethnicity in India is expressed in terms of language, religion, caste, tribe, race and region. Ethnic groups in India broadly cover: dispersed linguistic and religious minorities; immigrants, outsiders and refugees; marginal and peripheral communities; and smaller tribal and indigenous groups not worthy of being organised in sovereign or provincial terms. As far as ethnicity is concerned, there is no much problem for Indian nation. Ethnic conflicts do not as such threaten the unity and integrity of Indian nation, although they influence social harmony and integration to a great extent. These ethnic conflicts are 'communal' or in the nature of inter-group clashes and they can be effectively managed through good governance and balanced economic development by the institutions of the State.

So far as regional nationalism is concerned, four different types are noticed in India: autonomist, separatist, irredentist and secessionist. Of these, the secessionist types only pose serious threats as they involve the break-up of the Indian nation. The autonomist and separatist types are province-seeking nationalism and hence they do not pose much threat to the Indian nation. These forms of regional nationalism exist in India since the colonial times and the main goal of this nationalism is to secure self-rule for a distinct cultural nation within the provisions of a provincial unit within the Indian Union (Nanda, 2006). The post-colonial Indian State has accommodated most of these regional nationalisms by granting provincial statehoods to the concerned cultural nations on populist grounds.

Ethnicity and Nation-building: The North Eastern Situation

As a distinct and strategically located geo-political entity, the North Eastern region of India came into being after the partition of colonial India in 1947. At that time, the region covered the erstwhile province of Assam and the Part C princely States of Manipur, Tripura and the Khasi tribes. At present, the region comprises the geographically contiguous States of Arunachal Pradesh, Assam, Manipur, Meghalaya, Mizoram, Nagaland, Tripura—commonly referred to as 'seven sisters'—and the geographically isolated State of Sikkim. As its eighth member, Sikkim was officially included in the region in 2003; the northern areas of West Bengal separate Sikkim from the other North Eastern States.

The North Eastern region covers an area of 2, 62,179 sq. km, which accounts for 7.9 per cent of the total area of India. The population of the region stands at 39,035,582, which constitutes 3.8 per cent of the total Indian population (Census of India, 2001). Ninety-eight per cent of the boundary of the region is international border shared by China's Tibet region and Bhutan on the north, Myanmar on the east and the south and Bangladesh on the west and the south. With mainland India, the region is linked with a 37 km long small corridor of land, popularly called the 'chicken's neck'. The region is a biodiversity hotspot because of its floral and faunal diversity. It is also a cultural hotspot because of its overwhelming cultural and ethnic diversity. Hill areas cover 70 per cent of the region and the rest is covered by valleys formed by the Bramhaputra, Barak and Imphal rivers. Both non-tribal and tribal people inhabit the region and their cultures combine the traits of both 'Indic Asia' and 'Asiatic Asia'. The non-tribal people mainly populate the valley areas and the tribal people primarily live in the hill areas of the region. The average density of the region is 149, which is much lower than the all-India average of 313. The literacy rate of the region is 68.5 per cent and the urban population stands at 15.45 per cent of the total population (Census of India, 2001).

The socio-cultural situation of the region is plural. More than 200 languages or mother tongues are spoken in the region. However, some of these languages have less than 10,000 speakers and hence are not listed in the 114 Indian languages classified by the 1991 census of India. Of the classified languages in the region, five languages, viz, Assamese, Bengali, Nepali, Manipuri (Meitei) and Bodo are scheduled languages. The first three belong to the Indo-Aryan and the last two belong to the Tibeto-Burmese linguistic family. Again, as scheduled languages, Assamese, Manipuri and Bodo are native to the region; whereas Bengali and Nepali are spoken in other parts of India as well. The Assamese language has nearly 20 million speakers, followed by Bengali with a sizeable number (nearly 10 million) of speakers. Apart from these two languages, Manipuri has 1.3 million, Bodo 1.2 million, Khasi 1.1 million, Garo 1.0 million and Mizo nearly 1.0 million speakers. The other distinct languages of the region such as Tripuri, Miri/Mishing, Karbi/Mikir, Nepali, Ao, Nissi/Dafla, Sema, Adi, Rabha, Konyak, Tangkhul, Angami, Dimasa, Lotha, Mao, Kabui, Kuki, Chakesang, Phom, Bishnupriya, Koch, Zeliang, Nocte, etc., have speakers ranging between few thousands or lakhs. The Naga tribes have adopted a *lingua franca* called 'Nagamese', but this has not been recorded by the census. Most of the languages in North Eastern region are associated with a traditional or adopted homeland. For example, Assamese is associated with Assam; Bengali with Tripura and the Cachar region of Assam; Manipuri with Manipur; Bodo with the Bodo areas in lower Assam; Karbi / Mikir with Karbi-Anglong hills; Dimasa with North Cachar hills of Assam; Khasi with Khasi hills; Garo with Garo hills of Meghalaya; Mizo with Mizoram; Ao, Sema, Konyak, Angami, Lotha, Tangkhul, Mao, Kabui etc., with Naga hills.

As far as the religious composition is concerned, almost all the major and minor religions of India as well as scores of tribal religions exist in the region. The non-tribal people in the region mainly follow Hinduism; whereas Christianity is popular among the tribal people. The States of Assam, Tripura, Sikkim and Manipur are Hindu majority States; but the Christian tribes dominate the States of Meghalaya, Mizoram and Nagaland. Nearly 50 per cent of the tribes of the region follow Christianity. The Christian tribals account for 87.44 per cent in Nagaland, 85.65 per cent in Mizoram, 64.56 per cent in Meghalaya and 34.14 per cent in Manipur. The Hindus account for 67.13 per cent in Assam, 86.51 per cent in Tripura, 68.47 per cent in Sikkim,

57.65 per cent in Manipur and 36.99 per cent in Arunachal. The Muslims in Assam constitute 28.43 per cent, in Tripura 7.29 per cent and in Manipur 7.11 per cent of the population. Buddhism in the region is mainly found in Sikkim and Arunachal; in the former, the Buddhists constitute 27.09 per cent and in the latter 12.83 per cent. Most of the tribes in Arunachal also practice their traditional tribal religions. Apart from this, small number of Jains, Sikhs and Bahai' faith people also exist in the region. The tribal people of the region account for 25.8 per cent of the total population. Out of the 450 Indian tribes, nearly 200 tribes are found in the region. Only 120 tribes and sub-tribes have been given the scheduled tribe status. The scheduled tribes in Mizoram form 94.75 per cent, in Nagaland 87.61 per cent and in Meghalaya 85.5 per cent of the population (Government of Meghalaya, 2004).

The multiplicity of linguistic, religious and tribal groups produced enormous cultural and ethnic identities in the North Eastern region. Like elsewhere in India, cultural nations in the region are also formed due to the strong association of language, culture and tribe with specific geographical spaces. Some of the territorially rooted linguistic and tribal communities of the region are large enough (i.e. having population more than one million) to be politically organised in autonomous or independent terms. In other words, they are politically capable of becoming self-ruling and self sustaining units and hence qualify for the term nation in the cultural sense. But some of the tribal groups with specific home territory in the region are very small enough (i.e. having population in few thousands or lakhs) to be self-sustaining and self-ruling in autonomous or independent terms and hence are reduced to the status of ethnic groups. Going by this logic, the Assamese, the Bengalis (particularly in Tripura and to some extent in Cachar), the Nagas, the Manipuris (Meiteis), the Bodos, the Khasis, the Mizos, the Garos can be termed as cultural nations; whereas the smaller tribal groups such as the Mishings, Karbis, Adis, Nissis, Rabhas, Reangs, Kukis, Kochs, Chakmas, Jamatias, Monpas, Noctes, Lalungs, Dimasas, Ahoms, Morans, Chutiyas, Mattocks, Tangkhuls, Kabuis, Bishnupriyas, Zeliangs, etc., whose population range from less than 10,000 to nearly 5,00,000, can be termed as ethnic groups. The Nagas, comprising nearly 30 tribes, represent a unique situation in North East India. Although, each Naga tribe is a small distinct group with a population ranging between 10,000 to 200,000 persons, yet, together they constitute a cultural nation based on common tribal identity and specific geographic space and a population of 1.8 million.

Apart from the smaller tribal groups, migration from various parts of India and from across the international border, especially from Bangladesh and to some extent from Nepal, in different periods of time contributed to a large extent to the formation of ethnic groups in the North East. Migration to the region dates back to 12th century. Nevertheless, the early migrants turned themselves into natives and indigenous people; whereas some recent migrants, especially who came in the colonial and post-colonial times, remained as ethnic groups. The colonial rulers brought several people to the North East from different parts of India to work in the oil, tea, rubber, coal industries as well as to assist them in administration, trade and commerce. The descendants of these people in most cases turned into ethnic groups (e.g. the ethnic Tea Tribes and the ethnic Bengalis). Further, the series of migration resulted by the 1947 partition and the Indo-Pak war of 1971 contributed to more ethnic formations in the region. The ethnic population also resulted from the migration of people from other parts of India due to the expansion of administration, transport and communication, business, trade and industry in the region after independence. The formation of 'protected tribal lands' and the new provinces in the region also led to creation of minorities who became ultimately ethnic groups. Continuous illegal migration, or infiltration after 1971, also added to ethnic formations in the region.

It is thus clear that the North Eastern region contains distinct cultural nations as well as ethnic groups; the latter consisting of smaller tribal groups, scattered minorities, immigrants, outsiders and marginal groups. Given this situation, the Indian State should primarily focus on accommodating these diverse cultural nations and ethnic groups within the multicultural or plural framework of nation-building. The Indian State, since independence, adopted a series of political and cultural measures for nation- building in the region. The first step in this direction was the integration of the native States of Manipur, Tripura and Khasi tribes. This move was part of the larger scheme of integration of 562 princely States with the Indian Union during 1947-49. The next move was the creation of Autonomous District Council (ADC) in

1952 for certain tribal areas under the Sixth Schedule of the Indian Constitution based on the recommendations of the Bordoloi sub-committee set up by the Constituent Assembly in 1946. Most of these areas formed 'excluded' and 'partially excluded' areas in colonial times. Under the Sixth Schedule, ADCs are formed for the Kahsi-Jaintia, Garo, Karbi-Mikir, Dimasa, Lai, Mara, Chakma and Tripuri tribal groups. As local self-governing bodies, these ADCs enjoy Constitutional rights, powers and privileges to protect and promote tribal autonomy, cultural identity, customary laws and practices and the matters relating to public employment, ownership and inheritance of property, elected offices, etc. But, some people argue that the district councils have created excusive tribal enclaves which resulted in ethnic clashes between tribal and non-tribal people. These clashes in most cases lead to internal displacement of people from their own lands, which in turn create further ethnic formations (Baruah, 2003).

In 1954, Manipur and Tripura were formed into union territories and the Abor, Tirap Hills and Naga Tribal areas and Tuensang were constituted into North Eastern Frontier Tract. The same year, Lushai Hills became Mizo Hills District. But during the first major States reorganisation in India in 1956, the North Eastern region was not touched. At that time, some major States in South India were created following primarily the principle of linguistic uniformity and cultural homogeneity. This principle was not applied to the North Eastern situation, as most of individual tribal groups were very small in number. However, as the unity and integrity of the Indian State was threatened by the armed struggle for Naga independence and by the Chinese aggression of 1962, the State of Nagaland was formed in 1963. This was done to pacify Naga secessionist nationalism, on the one hand, and to accommodate the autonomous existence of Naga identity within the Indian Union, on the other. In the formation of Nagaland State, the authorities did not follow the criteria of linguistic uniformity, economic soundness and financial viability. Thereafter, the North Eastern Frontier Agency (NEFA) was formed under the Ministry of External Affairs in 1965.

Nagaland was the first small as well as tribal State in India and its formation led to the rise of tribal nationalisms in the region demanding either independent or provincial statehood. Three years after the formation of Nagaland, Mizo nationalism movement, calling for an independent State, kicked off in Mizo hills. Besides, the Khasi, Jaintia, Garo and Karbi tribes together, under the banner of All Party Hill Leaders Conference (APHLC), agitated for the creation of a hill State for them. In view of the rising tribal nationalist movements, the North-Eastern Areas (Reorganisation) Act was passed in 1971. Based on this Act, the North-Eastern Council (NEC) for the development of the region was formed in 1971 and the State of Meghalaya comprising the Khasi, Jaintia and Garo tribes was formed in 1972. The same year, the union territories of Manipur and Tripura were granted full statehood and the Mizo hills district and NEFA were made into the union territories of Mizoram and Arunachal Pradesh, respectively (Kumar, 1998). Following this Act, the expression 'North Eastern region' becomes distinct in the Indian official vocabulary and administrative lexicon. After twenty years of armed struggle, Mizo nationalism finally reconciled for autonomy, and accordingly, the State of Mizoram came into being in 1987; the same year Arunachal Pradesh also became a full-fledged State. With this, most of the hill districts of erstwhile Assam became provincial States. But the demands for more States such as Bodoland, Karbi-Anglong, Rabhaland, Kamtapur, Cachar, Garoland, Kukiland and Zeliangrong continue unabated in the region. To accommodate the Bodo aspiration, the Bodoland Autonomous Council (BAC) was formed in 1996 and later the Bodoland Territorial Council (BTC) was formed in 2003. Now, it is renamed as the Bodoland Territorial Area Districts (BTAD). Recently, the demand for Kamtapur State has become very active; the All Koch Rajbongsi Students Union (AKRSU) launched widespread agitation and organised road blockade for fulfilment of the demand.

Along with the above political moves, some cultural measures of nation-building in the region have been also taken. These measures *inter alia* include : recognition of the Constitutional rights (Art. 29 and 30) to the regional linguistic groups to preserve their language and the religious minorities to establish educational institutions; the Constitutional provision of 'protective discrimination' (Art. 22) to the scheduled tribes of the region; protection of customary laws, traditional practices and social institutions of some tribes under the Sixth Schedule; and recognition of traditional tribal councils and tribal advisory councils in the Fifth Schedule areas of the region. However, some sections of the population of the region, such as, the Ahom, Chutiya, Moran, Mattock, Koch Rajbongsi and Tea Tribes are still demanding for their inclusion in the scheduled tribe category. Because, inclusion in the scheduled category implies socio-economic advantages in the matter of education, public employment and elected office (Baruah, 2007). The Ahom, Moran, Reang also clamour for district council under the Sixth Schedule. Similarly, the Khasi, Garo and Mizo tribes are demanding for inclusion of their languages in the Eighth Schedule. These political and cultural measures undertaken by the Indian State clearly reflect the multicultural approach of nation-building and any departure from this will not be welcomed.

The nation-building process in North East India is not free from challenges. The challenges primarily come from two sources: (a) regional nationalisms by various tribal and non-tribal people; and (b) ethnic conflicts and clashes. As already mentioned, four different types of regional nationalism—autonomist, separatist, irredentist and secessionist—are seen in India. All these forms of regional nationalism are noticed in North East India to a great extent. Like other parts of India, the autonomist and separatist type of regional nationalism in the North East are primarily concerned with establishing culture-congruent provincial or politico-administrative spaces within the Indian Union (e.g., the demands for provincial States like Bodoland, Garoland, Kamtapur, Rabhaland, etc., by different tribes of the region). The irredentist type is concerned with integrating the outlying areas of a nationality within its provincial boundary (e.g. the Assam-Meghalaya border dispute or the 'Greater Nagaland' issue). The secessionist type of regional nationalism in the region (e.g. Naga nationalism, etc.) mainly aims at independence of the concerned regional nationality from the Indian State. The secessionist nationalism sees nation in the context of sovereignty only and hence attainment of a sovereign State remains its main ideology and goal.

The autonomist and separatist types of regional nationalism in the region do not pose serious challenges to the process of nation-building in India precisely because they do not threaten the territorial unity and integrity of the Indian State. As these regional nationalisms clearly reflect the fulfilment of people's aspiration within the legal-political framework of the Indian Constitution, they can be politically accommodated by granting provincial statehood or any form of autonomy or self-ruling institution within the Indian Union. The irredentist regional nationalism, however, poses much problem for nation-building as it involves inclusion of areas from different provinces. For example, the 'Greater Nagaland' demand includes Naga areas from the States of Manipur, Assam and Arunachal Pradesh. In response to this demand, widespread violence was seen in Manipur in 2003-04 (Hussain and Routray, 2001). The secessionist nationalisms in the region offer the most serious challenges to the process of nation-building in India (Nag, 2002). Interestingly, most of the regional nationalisms in the North East have tended to develop secessionist goal.

It is fairly well known that the Naga national movement, which began in 1946, is the first and foremost secessionist nationalist movement in the region. It continues even today, though dormant since 1997 because of the peace talks with the Indian government. The secessionist Naga leadership perceives the Nagas, who comprise a group of nearly 30 disparate tribes, as a nation in sovereign sense, and hence it presses for their right to self-determination in sovereign terms (Srikanth and Thomas, 2005). It rejected autonomy under the Sixth Schedule as well as self-determination in terms of provincial Nagaland State and indulged in armed struggle against the Indian State to achieve a sovereign Naga State. Since 1980s, the Isak-Muivah faction and the Khaplang faction of the National Socialist Council of Nagaland (NSCN) have been playing the vanguard role of Naga nationalism and both the factions, though engaged in peace talks, are persistent with their sovereignty demand (Ao, 2002).

In Manipur, the United National Liberation Front (UNLF) and a few more insurgent and militant organisations lead the secessionist Meitei nationalism since 1960. Contesting the integration of Manipur with the Indian Union, these rebel groups fight for the establishment of an independent Manipur State (Verghese, 1997). Mizo secessionist nationalism, which emerged in 1966 to achieve a sovereign Mizo State, changed its trajectory and accepted autonomy for Mizo nationality in provincial sense. Secessionist form of Assamese nationalism emerged with the formation of United Liberation Front of Asom (ULFA) in 1979. Raising the issue of illegal migrants and infiltrators, the ULFA spearheaded an armed struggle for achievement of a sovereign Assam (Egreteau, 2006). Apart from this, secessionist nationalism is also spearheaded by the National Democratic Front of Bodoland (NDFB) in the Bodo area, the Achik National Volunteer Council (ANVC) in the Garo hills, the Hynniewtrep National Liberation Council (HNLC) in the Khasi hills and the United People's Democratic Solidarity (UPDS) in Karbi-Anglong and North Cachar hills of Assam. Thus, except Sikkim and Arunachal Pradesh, the rest of the North Eastern States are marred by either province seeking nationalism or secessionist nationalism. It is important to note that the method of agitation characterised by insurgency, militancy and armed struggle is common to both province-seeking and sovereign State-seeking regional nationalism in the region.

The ethnic conflicts in the region are seen in the form of tribal-non-tribal, tribal-tribal, native-outsiders and settlers-migrants conflicts. In Assam, ethnic conflict is seen recently in Bodo area between the Bodos and the ethnic Santhalis belonging to the 'Adivasi' or 'Tea Tribe' category (Bhan, 1999). Ethnic conflicts are also seen in Upper Assam between smaller tribes or between the native Assamese and migrant Bengalis and the so-called 'Bihari' migrants. These ethnic conflicts mainly result from the apprehensions of the natives of losing socio-economic opportunities in the face of increasing migrant population. The natives here play the 'sons of the soil' card to protect their interest and to drive the migrants out of their land. In response, the Tea Tribes formed All Adivasi Students Association (AASA) and Adivasi National Liberation Army (ANLA) to protect their interest. The most significant and protracted ethnic conflict seen in the region is the fight of the native Assamese people against the ethnic Bengalis, especially the Bengali Muslims and the illegal Bangladeshi migrants. The majority Assamese Hindus also conflict with the minority Assamese Muslims; the latter recently formed the Assam United Democratic Front (AUDF) and the Assam Minority Students Union (AMSU) to protect them from the majority onslaught.

The Assamese-Bengali ethnic conflicts date back to the post-partition and post-1971 periods. Widespread skirmishes between the two communities erupted when Assamese was declared as the official language in 1960 and as the medium of instruction in 1970. But the most serious conflicts were seen during the Assam agitation from 1979 to 1985 against the illegal Bengali Muslim migrants and the Bangladeshis. Spearheaded mainly by the All Assam Students Union (AASU) and the Asom Gana Sangram Parishad (AGSP), the conflict mainly focused on the detection and deportation of these illegal migrants (Hussain, 1993; Baruah, 1999). The agitation continues till today and the AASU, supported by the Asom Jatiyatabadi Yuva Chhatra Parishad (AJYCP), these days insist on the implementation of the Assam Accord of 1985 and the setting up of tribunals under Illegal Migrants (Detection by Tribunals) Act. The Assam government recently set up 21 tribunals for the detection and deportation of illegal migrants. It has been recently revealed that there are nearly 1.2 million illegal infiltrators (or Bangladeshis) in Assam. The illegal infiltration mainly takes place at the porous borders in Dhubri and Karimganj districts of Assam. However, the identification of these migrants becomes a real problem as the language, culture and even the religion between the legal citizens and the foreigners are common. Ethnic conflicts between different tribal groups such as the Kuki and Naga, Meitei and Naga, Meitei and Bishnupriya, Kuki and Paite, Dimasa and Karbi, Kuki and Karbi, Khasi and Karbi are seen in different parts of the region. Further, the conflicts between Mizos and Reangs (Dutta, 2005) as well as Tripuri tribes and Bengalis (Barpujari, 1998) are some of the other instances of ethnic conflict in the region. The ethnic conflicts in the region unlike secessionist nationalisms do not cause any major threat to the territorial unity and integrity of the region; they mostly impair peace and stability, jeopardise social harmony and integration, and create distrust and negative attitude.

In sum, it can be said that like any other part of India, ethnic groups differ from cultural nations in the North Eastern context. As noted earlier, ethnicity in the North Eastern context has to be referred to mean migrants, outsiders, smaller tribal groups and marginal groups. The nation-building efforts followed by the Indian State in the North Eastern context should acknowledge the distinction between ethnic groups and cultural nations and should not dub all the cultural communities of the region as ethnic groups from the point of view of the Indian State. Calling all the cultural communities of the region as ethnic groups presupposes interpretation of nation-building in terms of the nation-state principle or the mainstream community perspective.

The nation-building in North East India should accommodate all the cultural nations and ethnic groups following the multi-cultural perspective. The adoption of the political and cultural measures since independence and the formation of the seven North Eastern States are clear indications of multicultural perspective of nation-building and any forceful or otherwise attempt from the mainstream perspective of nation-building should be avoided for good. The threats to nation-building in the North Eastern region come mainly from the imposition of the nation-state or mainstream perspective as well as the incidence of secessionist national movements. The latter can be effectively managed within the multicultural framework of nation-building.

Conclusion

To conclude, it can be argued that the whole population of a multi-cultural State like India constitutes nation in political or civic sense and such a political nation consists of both cultural nations and ethnic groups. An ethnic group is basically a group of people dissociated from its ancestral or adopted homeland; it is a group which follows its distinct culture but lives outside its home territory. In addition, ethnic groups also include the smaller marginal or peripheral tribal groups and indigenous groups. A cultural nation is basically a cultural community anchored to an ancestral or adopted homeland; it may or may not exist with a State of its own. Sovereignty is not the quintessential feature of a cultural nation; a cultural nation can exist without being endowed with sovereignty. Cultural nations in India are formed based on language, tribe, and to some extent, on religion.

The nation-state approach of nation-building in its quest for uniformity tries to homogenise the cultural nations and ethnic groups in India in terms of the language, culture and religion of the majority or mainstream community. But this approach is not appropriate for Indian situation. What is appropriate for Indian situation is a multicultural or multi-national perspective of nation-building which emphasises the civil perspective of nation at the all-India level and the cultural perspective of nation at the regional level. In other words, nation-building approach in India should focus on accommodating all the diverse cultural-national and ethnic identities under the common Indian polity. The recognition of 22 scheduled languages, the classification of

114 mother tongues and the guarantee of religious freedom and the secular character of Indian State strongly establish the plural identity of Indian nation. Hence, any effort for the mainstream perspective of nation-building implying 'Hindiisation' or 'Hinduisation' of the Indian people will meet with crisis and turbulence in different parts of India. Being a multicultural country, India should always be conceptualised as a nation in political terms and not in cultural sense of the majority community. If at all India is viewed as a nation in cultural sense, it should be in multi-cultural or plural sense and not in mono-cultural sense. The recent coalition era in Indian politics, which began from 1996, is a clear endorsement and reflection of cultural pluralism and ethnic diversities in Indian society. If the coalition politics is anything to go by, then the multi-cultural perspective of nation- building in India cannot be replaced with any other perspective.

References

Ao, A. L. 2002. *From Phizo to Muivah: Naga National Question in Northeast India.* New Delhi: Mittal Publications.

Barpujari, H. K. 1998. *Northeast India: Problems, Policies and Prospects.* New Delhi: Spectrum Publication.

Barth, Frederick. 1969. *Ethnic Groups and Boundaries: The Social Organisation of Cultural Difference.* London: George Allen and Unwin.

Baruah, Sanjib. 1999. *India against Itself: Assam and the Politics of Nationality.* New Delhi: Oxford University Press.

Baruah, Sanjib. 2003. 'Citizens and denizens: Ethnicity, homelands and the crisis of displacement in Northeast India'. *Journal of Refugee Studies*, 16, 1: 44-66.

Baruah, Sanjib. 2007. *Post Frontier Blues: Toward a New Policy Framework for Northeast India.* Washington: East-West Centre, Policy Studies No. 33.

Bhan, Susheela. 1999. *Impact of Ethnic Violence on Youth: A Study of Tribal-Nontribal Violence in Kokrajhar, Assam.* New Delhi: Shipra Publications.

Brass, Paul. 1974. *Language, Religion and Politics in North India.* New Delhi: Vikas Publishing House.

Cashmore, Ellis E. 1984. *Dictionary of Race and Ethnic Relations.* London: Routledge and Kegan Paul.

Cohen, Abner. 2004. *Urban Ethnicity.* London: Sage Publications.

Connor, Walker. 1972. 'Nation-building or nation-destroying?' *World Politics.* 24, 3: 319-355.

Desai, A.R. 1966. *Social Background of Indian Nationalism.* Bombay: Popular Prakashan.

Dutta, S.K. 2005. *Uprooted Reangs: Strangers in their Motherland.* New Delhi: Akansha.

Egreteau, Renaud. 2006. *Instability at the Gate: India's Troubled Northeast and its External Connections.* New Delhi: CHS Occasional Paper No. 16.

Eriksen, T.H. 2002. *Ethnicity and Nationalism: Anthropological Perspectives.* London: Pluto Press.

Ganguly, Rajat and Ian Macduff. 2003. *Ethnic Conflict and Secessionism in South and South East Asia: Causes, Dynamics and Solutions.* New Delhi: Sage Publications.

Geertz, Clifford. 1971. 'The integrative revolution: Primordial solutions and civil politics'. In Clifford Geertz (Ed.): *Old Societies and New States.* pp. 47-63, New Delhi: Amerind.

Glazer, Nathan and D. P. Moynihan. 1975. *Ethnicity: Theory and Experience.* Cambridge: Harvard University Press.

Government of India. 1991. *Census of India.*

Government of India. 2001. *Census of India.*

Government of Meghalaya. 2004. *Where Do We Stand in Northeast in 2003?* Shillong: Directorate of Economics and Statistics.

Guha, Amalendu. 1983. 'Little Nationalism turned Chauvinist: Assam's anti-foreigner Upsurge (1970-80)'. *Economic and Political Weekly.* 5, Special Issue: 1701-1709.

Hayes, C. H. 2006. 'Nationalism'. In E. R. A. Seligman (Ed.): *Encyclopaedia of the Social Sciences.* Volume 11, Part. I. pp. 241-248, New Delhi: Cosmo Publications.

Hussain, Monirul. 1993. *The Assam Movement: Class, Ideology and Movement.* New Delhi: South Asian Books.

Hussain, Wasbir and B. P. Routray. 2001. 'Naga identity, Meitei nationalism and electoral politics: Sub-nationalism in Northeast India'. *South Asia Terrorism Portal.* New Delhi: Institute of Conflict Management.

Isaac, Harold. 1975. *Idols of the Tribe: Group Identity and Political Change.* New York: Harper.

Jenkins, Richard. 1997. *Rethinking Ethnicity: Arguments and Explorations.* London: Sage Publications.

Khan, Raseeduddin. 1987. *Composite Culture of India and National Integration.* New Delhi: Allied Publishers.

Khan, Raseeduddin. 1994. *Bewildered India: Identity, Pluralism and Discord.* New Delhi: Har-Anand Publications.

Kumar, B.B. 1998. *Small States Syndrome in India.* New Delhi: Concept Publishing Co.

Lesley, Brown. 1993. *The New Shorter Oxford English Dictionary.* Oxford: Clarendon Press.

Nag, Sajal. 2002. *Contesting Marginality: Ethnicity, Insurgency and Sub-nationalism in Northeast India.* New Delhi: Manohar.

Nanda, S.K. 2006. 'Cultural nationalism in a multinational context: The case of India'. *Sociological Bulletin.* 55, 1: 24-44.

Nanda, S.K. 2007. *Nationalism and Regionalism in India: The Case of Orissa.* Delhi: Kalpaz Publications.

Nigam, R.C., 1971, *Language Handbook of Mother Tongues in Census.* New Delhi: Office of the Registrar General of India.

Oommen, T.K. 1990. *State and Society in India: Studies in Nation-Building.* New Delhi: Sage Publications.

Oommen, T.K. 1996. 'State, nation and ethnic: The processual linkages'. In P. Radcliffe (Ed.): *Race, Ethnicity and Nation.* pp. 26-44, London: Routledge.

Parekh, Bhikhu. 2000. *Rethinking Multiculturalism: Cultural Diversity and Political Theory.* New York: Plagrave.

Phadnis, Urmilla. 1990. *Ethnicity and Nation-Building in South Asia.* New Delhi: Sage Publications.

Smith, Anthony D. 1986. *Ethnic Origins of Nations.* Oxford: Basil Blackwell.

Srikanth, H. and C. J. Thomas. 2005. 'Naga resistance movement and the peace process in Northeast India'. *Peace and Democracy in South Asia.* 1, 2: 57-87.

Verghese, B.G. 1997. *India's Northeast Resurgent: Ethnicity, Insurgency, Governance and Development.* New Delhi: Konark.

Vijapur, A. 1998. *Dimensions of Federal Nation-Building: Essays in Honour of Raseeduddin Khan.* New Delhi: Manak Publications.

Weber, Max. 1922. *Economy and Society Vol. II* (Eds.) Gwenth, Roth and Clause Wittich. 1978. Berkeley: University of California Press.

3 Customary Laws and Tribal Identity in North Eastern India

Walter Fernandes

Studies on conflicts in the North East indicate that while economic and political issues are crucial, the search for an identity is basic for their understanding. The customary law is central to this search of most tribal communities. That explains why the Naga and Mizo accords included its recognition by introducing Articles 371A and 371G in the Constitution. However, interaction with modernity in the form of education, religious change and the formal law has affected the tribes in general and their customary law in particular. This chapter will discuss the impact of this interface on their identity.

The Background of the Changes

Studies on social change in the North East indicate that modernisation of tribal societies without preparing them to deal with its possible ill effects can strengthen patriarchy and result in class formation. Their community ownership-based equity and the relatively high status, accorded by most customary laws, to their womenfolk without making them equal to men, are intrinsic to their culture and identity. However, their laws have to interact with the predominantly male-oriented, individual ownership-based formal legal, social and political systems of the country. This tradition-modernity interface has influenced their customary laws. Some tribal leaders react to this interface by demanding that their tradition be kept intact, a few accept the dominant value system and abandon their tradition as outdated while a third group goes back to their customary law to reinterpret according to the norms of the formally system by giving it a strong male orientation (Fernandes *et al.*, 2005: 38-40). All these reactions can go against the tribe in general and women in particular. Instead, ways have to be found of dealing with this interface without their adverse impact on women and equity.

What goes against women's relatively high status or equity are bound to have a negative impact on their culture and identity.

The present chapter is based on a comparative study on the gender impact of the evolution of tribal customary laws (Fernandes *et al.*, 2005). Since the reaction of each tribe depends on the extent of changes it experiences in its tradition, the study was done among five tribes that were at different stages of modernisation. The Dimasa and Garo, who come under the Sixth Schedule that recognizes community ownership (CPRs), have to interact with the individual-based formal law (Bordoloi, 1984). The Aka are close to their tradition and governed by their customary law but the Sixth Schedule does not apply to them. Article 371A recognizes the Angami customary law, but there are indications that because of their interface with modernity, men interpret it in their own favour (D'Souza and Kekhrieseno, 2003: 33-34). The *Adibasi* whose ancestors came from Middle India as indentured labour in the Assam tea gardens, have for all practical purposes lost their customary law and tribal identity and represent one of the most negative aspects of modernisation (Sharma and Kar, 1993: 133-135).

The study that combined individual interviews and group discussions with participant observation, and compared their present and past, showed the impact of various degrees of exposure to modernity. The sample was 100 families from each tribe. In each family, one person was chosen as the main respondent. While interviewing the 244 male and 256 female main respondents, the views of other family members were recorded separately and used extensively in data analysis. The individual interviews were preceded by three group discussion sessions in each village. The demographic, educational and occupational status of the respondents was studied because they have a gender dimension.

Access to Modern Inputs

That modernity has affected the tribal communities is obvious but the study showed that its impact on the customary laws and on women is not uniform. Some changes have been supportive of class and gender equity and others are less so because of differential access to modern inputs such as education, religious change, commercial forces, administrative and financial systems that expose them to processes and communities outside their own. For example, education that is crucial to modernisation is linked also to religious change. Literacy is high among the Angami and Garo, a majority of whom gained access to schools after their Christianisation (Sanyu, 1996: 94-96). It is low among the rest.

Because of their relatively high level of education, many Angami and Garo tribals also hold jobs in the administration and the rest of the formal sector. As a result, the proportion of cultivators is low among them. Another cause of the low proportion of cultivators among the Garo is high landlessness and impoverishment. Many of them are daily wage earners. Thus, the occupations of the Garo show class formation in the tribe. Its causes will be analysed later. The proportion of cultivators is low also among the *Adibasi* but for different reasons. Most of them are tea garden workers who have not had access to education and are landless. Thus, the phenomenon of low proportion of cultivators; shows two different facets of modernisation. Among the Angami and a section of the Garo, it is the result of relatively high access to its benefits. The *Adibasi* and a section of the Garo show its negative implications (Fernandes *et al.,* 2005: 58-62).

Most Dimasa men as well as women are cultivators. However, there was difference between the 2004 study on changing land relations done in the harvesting season and the one on the customary law done after it. In the former, no Dimasa woman gave her occupation as housewife (Fernandes and Pereira, 2005: 94) but several of them reported this occupation in the latter. The women plays an important role in tribal agriculture, especially in *jhum.* In fact, shifting cultivation that is the main form among the Dimasa is called women's economy. From the big number of "housewives" among them, we assumed that in the harvesting season, they perceive themselves as cultivators but after it, their work is limited to the family and they consider themselves as housewives. However, after interviewing them again in order to understand this anomaly, we included all of them except old and pregnant women among cultivators because the second set of interviews showed that what has changed is not the objective reality but their self-perception.

Commercial crops are the basis of this changed perception. Those who have started growing them continue to be as active in their cultivation as in the *jhum* operations. However, they have come to believe that, they get monetary income from the commercial crops when they are actually involved in their cultivation because money comes immediately after it. They do not think of themselves as economic assets when they are not involved in it directly outside the agricultural season. *Jhum*, on the contrary, is a full cycle. In the agricultural season, they cultivate the crops they need for the year and use them after the harvest (Fernandes *et al.*, 2005: 34). Thus, the transition to commercial crops has changed their self-perception but their customary law continues to govern their society. A certain disjunction has thus appeared between their economic and social lives. Unlike in *jhum* in which they are economic asset in and outside the season, in the money-based commercial crops they consider themselves economically active only when they are actual producers, not outside the season.

This change has implications for their identity as noticed also in an earlier study among Angami women. In their tradition, she was in charge of children's education while men trained boys into adulthood. Girls did not have access to education since it belonged to the social sphere (Vitso, 1998: 7-8). However, at the height of the Naga Nationalist struggle in the 1970s, a large number of young men went into hiding leaving women in charge of their family and society. That is when schools came to the southern Angami area and girls gained access to them. As a result, 41 out of 68 graduates in the families studied were women. However, that did not change the male orientation of their customary law. 131 out of 168 persons having salaried jobs were men, because the State, the main employer views men alone as breadwinners and gives them priority in jobs. Besides, a large number of Angami women remain unmarried since their tradition demands that the husband be better educated than the wife is and the tribe does not have enough educated men (Fernandes and Barbora, 2002: 85-86; 111-113).

The Customary Law and the Family

Modernisation seen in this perspective strengthens the patriarchal character of their customary law. This change has affected also the family sphere because of the importance money has assumed. The women continue to be in charge of discipline in the family. When herbs abounded, she took care of the family health needs but today most tribal families have switched over to allopathic medicine or combine religious rites with it. Since it involves money, the decisions about health care are shifting to men (D'Souza and Kekhrieseno, 2003: 33-34). *Adibasi* women continue to be in charge of health care because they do not have enough money for allopathic medicines and depend on herbs.

Education too is an interface with society. In their tradition, the child's socialisation was the woman's role assigned to women. The man trained boys into adulthood. Modern education requires money which, some like the Angami and the Dimasa, earn by growing cash crops. In the case of the Angami, it was a second crop of potatoes. Since they had this source, they had preserved their forests when their neighbours were destroying them. However, they began to cut forests in order to earn money when their sons attained the college going age (D'Souza, 2006: 50-51). That, together with the priority they gave to boys by sending them outside the region changed their culture, natural resource management and gender relations. When money is involved, decisions on education shift to men. Even when men do not decide it directly, they choose the commercial crops to grow and the mode of selling them. Thus, decisions in agriculture shift from women to men (Zehol, 1998: 21-22). Parents have also to decide how best to spend their money. They send both boys and girls to the primary school but since they do not have enough money to send all of them to college, they invest it on boys since as an *Adibasi* respondent said, they will remain at home while girls will go away after marriage. Because of the situation described above, most Angami boys and girls have equal access also to college. But some parents claim that, they give their daughters the gift of education and that they take their qualifications as property to their husband's house. Therefore, they should not demand inheritance rights (Fernandes *et al.,* 2005: 49-50).

Customary Law and Social Customs

Jhum is considered women's economy because unlike in settled agriculture in which the man owns land and takes all decisions concerning the crops and division of work, *jhum* has a gender friendly division of work. In most tribal traditions, the village council made up of men alone decide which plot to cultivate that year, what area to allot to each family according to the number of mouths to feed, which family with excess labour would help which one with labour shortage and the day before which work could not begin. After it, the man chose the plot his family would cultivate and performed the pre-cultivation rituals. At that stage, the woman took charge of production and divided work (Menon, 1995: 98-99). The women friendly division of work is true also of terrace cultivation (D'Souza, 2006: 21) but men tend to take charge of commercial crops and of market-oriented activities (Marak, 1997: 25-26).

One sees this changeover among the Aka. Traditionally, decisions about handicrafts depended on their type because they did not sell them. Therefore, they considered irrelevant the question of who took the decision on what handicrafts to produce. They had divided work between men and women according to the type of handicrafts and that division depended not on the sale value of the product but the use it was put to (Sinha, 1962). In their tradition, a village used to appoint one or two women to take the agricultural surplus and other goods to the plains for barter or sale. Today, intermediaries from the plains have entered the arena and the Aka sell their agricultural produce, handicrafts or other goods through them. Because of it, men have taken charge of sales and dealings with them because women among them have less exposure to the market economy than men do (Fernandes and Barbora, 2002: 128-130).

The biggest changes are in the marriage that is a social reproduction system and an interface with society. Some tribes had fixed partners. For example, the Garo heir had to marry her father's nephew. Where the partners were not fixed, marriage was through personal choice or arranged with the help of mediators. Most tribes also had the system of marriage by elopement. Some like the Aka did not give much choice to the girl and even had child marriage. Among those who were allowed a choice, once the partners were fixed, some boys and girls got the mother's permission and others of both the parents but in every case, they approached the father through the mother who was the decision-maker in the family. After her approval, the father took the decision to the village council for its consent. After it, some tribes allowed the boy and girl to live together as man and wife. The formal marriage came much later depending on the convenience of the family (Goswami, 1986).

These customs have changed mainly because of religious change and commercial influences. Education is the main cause of inter-community marriages that are not uncommon. Where women have had better access to education than boys, many girls remain unmarried or marry outside the tribe since there are not enough educated boys who can keep the norm that they be better educated than girls (Fernandes and Barbora, 2002: 86-87). Only some *Adibasi,* all of them of the older generation, had followed the custom of the boy and girl living together after getting the consent of the village council. The ban on pre-marital co-habitation comes from their Christianisation or Hinduisation. The Aka have in practice banned child marriage and have given a new interpretation to bride price. In the past, it was perceived as the man compensating the family that lost a worker. Today some Aka women want to ban bride price because many men view the *mithuns* and other items they give to the bride's father as a price paid for her. Women fear that it turns her into a commodity. Bride price exists also among the Dimasa but not with the new Aka interpretation.

Formalisation of marriage too has changed. Formerly, social and religious recognition came from the consent of the village council and the rituals performed by the tribal priest (Goswami, 1985). Today, Angami and Garo Christians get religious recognition and have their marriage formalised in the church. Most Dimasa and *Adibasi* have been hinduised and go through temple rituals. However, both Christians and Hindus perform their traditional rituals in their homes. Thus, religious change has in practice effected a separation between the religious and social spheres. The church and the temple give them religious sanction and their rituals grant them social recognition (Ruivah, 2002: 167).

Habitat change too differs with the tribe. The virilocal *Adibasi,* Aka and Angami have retained the custom of the woman joining the man's clan and the children belonging to it. Among the matrilocal Garo, the boy and the girl retain their original clan but the children belong to the mother's line. Forty-two out of the 82 Dimasa clans are matrilineal. In most clans, the man and the woman retain their clan. In the male descent clans, the child joins the father's clan and in the female descent, it belongs to the mother's clan. Similar rules are followed for the family name. However, even in the matrilineal clans, property remains with the man and that seems to be a relatively recent change. The Angami couple builds a new house on land allotted by the husband's father. In the past, the Dimasa husband spent some time in the girl's house before building a house close to it but they could not live in his parents' house. Today, the nuclear family is becoming the norm especially in the salaried class. Most of them build a house away from the parents of the couple. It has gender implications. While the couple has autonomy in a nuclear family, it can also deprive the woman of her family support (Goswami, 1982). The Garo are matrilocal. The sisters of the heir are allowed to live in her house until they build their own house. Today, some educated Garo young men with a salaried job are demanding a changeover to a patrilineal, virilocal society. Some of them are introducing it in a new form. They "take the bride home" to their nuclear family home in the town and give their own family name to their children (Fernandes *et al.*, 2005: 111-112).

Inheritance Rights

Inheritance too is linked to habitation. The Garo have female inheritance but they remain a patriarchal matrilineal tribe. The woman inherits property but her uncle's permission is required for its alienation. Further change has entered their tribes with the State encouraging commercial crops and giving loans and subsidies only to individual owners and heads of families understood as men. With it, there is a slow changeover to *pattas* in the name of men (Barbora, 2002). The CPR dependent Aka lack the very concept of individual ownership and by assumption, of inheritance. However, the control over the CPRs is in the hands of the village council made up of men alone. The remaining three tribes have different forms of male inheritance. The Angami woman cannot inherit clan property but her parents can gift her acquired land and she can inherit what belongs to her mother. If the man dies without a son, his inheritance goes to his closest male relative (Fernandes and Barbora, 2002: 115-116).

The Dimasa have male inheritance, but if a man dies without a son, his daughter can inherit his property (Barpujari, 1997). Some change is visible among a few who have individual *pattas.* It has often caused class formation since members of the elite appropriate community land but we also saw two cases of men with individual *pattas* dividing their property equally between sons and daughters. More importantly, the village recognised the change. The *Adibasi* justify male inheritance by saying that the girl goes to the husband's house while the boy remains at home and takes care of his parents (Fernandes *et al.*, 2005: 132-133).

All the tribes allow the girl to inherit movable property. Mostly, daughters share their mother's belongings and sons get the father's belongings. Some Angami men present a few items to the daughters by using the custom of the girl receiving gifts but others use the same custom to justify their exclusion by claiming that the education given to them is their "gift" and their qualifications are their property that they take with them. The Dimasa mother's belongings go to the daughters, the father's belongings to the sons and the common ones are divided between sons and daughters (Goswami, 1986).

Table 3.1
Change Demanded in Laws of Inheritance

Tribe	*No change*	*No. girls marry outside*	*50% to women*	*Yes, if unmarried*	*No. women inherit*	*No both inherit*	*Total*
AKA							
Male	38	8	6	0	0	1	53
Female	32	8	7	0	0	0	47
M + F	70	16	13	0	0	1	100
ADIBASI							
Male	0	0	34	0	0	0	34
Female	0	0	66	0	0	0	66
M + F	0	0	100	0	0	0	100
ANGAMI							
Male	46	2	5	0	0	0	53
Female	33	2	10	2	0	0	47
M + F	79	4	15	2	0	0	100
DIMASA							
Male	34	0	0	0	0	20	54
Female	27	0	1	0	0	18	46
M + F	61	0	1	0	0	38	100
GARO							
Male	27	0	0	0	23	0	50
Female	25	0	0	0	25	0	50
M + F	52	0	0	0	48	0	100
Grand Total	262	20	129	2	48	39	500

Many tribal women are demanding changes in inheritance but the degree of the demand differs (Table 3.1) according to their exposure to modern inputs. Among the matrilineal Garo, it has taken the form of some educated men asking for male inheritance and in the remaining tribes, some women demand equal property rights. Garo women are fighting against the demand from men, but of importance, is the fact that the demand comes mainly from educated men who think that male inheritance is the natural social system. Since women exposed to the forces of modernity articulate the demand for change, it is minimal among the Aka, Dimasa and others who have not felt the impact of education and other modern factors. Among the Aka who are close to their tradition and live by their customary law, only in recent years, some girls have started going to school. As a result, even women among them justify the right of the village council over the CPRs. Many Dimasa women feel that they are not treated unjustly and that male inheritance does not have an adverse impact on their status. The *Adibasi* have very little to inherit but the SHGs have helped some of their women to become aware of their rights while education has done the same to the Angami who have most benefits of modernisation. Thus, where women have felt some positive impacts of modernisation such as education and jobs, the demand for change is vigorous. It is either mute or non-existent among most others (Fernandes and Barbora, 2002: 186-187).

Political Systems

While components such as marriage and inheritance differ from tribe to tribe, common to all of them is total separation between the family and social spheres. The woman may take decisions like children's education or even inherit land as in matrilineal societies but social power is in the hands of men. Nowhere is it clearer than in their traditional political systems. Some have village councils and others have chiefs or clan elders. The office may be hereditary or by election, but in every case men govern their societies. In recent years, some tribes have given a small voice to women. For example, some Angami villages have admitted the president of the Women's Association to the village council but she cannot hope to become its president. The Garo heiress had some voice in decisions concerning their society though men controlled the village council. That voice has got weak with modernisation. Though education and their new religion taught them, equality and universal adult franchise gave women the right of vote, their tradition denies it to them. However, because of women's associations and other inputs some of them have become aware of their rights at least to a limited extent and have started voicing opinions in favour of their rights. The entry of one of their members into the Angami village council is its result but very few have gone beyond it. We found two women village chiefs among the Aka. They are daughter or daughter-in-law of powerful men or of those who continue to wield power in their tribe.

Some new bodies such as the Village Development Board, *Panchayats* and District Autonomous Council are based on universal franchise and the right of women and men to contest elections. Some also have reservations for women. In principle, women have a right to contest State Assembly and Parliament elections but very few tribal women have availed of this opportunity. The Meghalaya Assembly had its first woman legislator two decades ago. Today, it has three in 40. The Karbi DAC has elected a woman in 2007. The remaining tribes have not elected a single woman to the DAC or the State Assembly. Nagaland had a Rajya Sabha member in the 1970s and none after it. A woman who contested its last Assembly pole was defeated. Before the 2004 elections for its lone Lok Sabha seat, some women's organisations wanted to put up a candidate for it. However, they were dissuaded from doing it.

This limited participation is because of lack of awareness of their rights among some tribal women and resistance from men in some others. A major recent change is the 73rd Amendment that reserves a third of the seats and posts in the local bodies for women. Of the five tribes studied, only the Aka and *Adibasi* have *Panchayats* and for the first time in their history, women have become their members and even presidents, for example at Palizi. This legal provision does not apply to the Garo and Dimasa Sixth Schedule areas. The Angami run their civil affairs according to their customary law under Article 371A. These bodies remain male dominated (Nongbri, 1998: 236). Thus, the customary law is re-interpreted to suit men's needs and that has become an obstacle to gender equity.

Besides, one cannot be euphoric about a third of the *Panchayat* members being women. Legal changes do not result automatically in social transformation. A close look at the situation shows that women's power is restricted largely to the four walls of the *Panchayat Samiti* (Banu, 2001: 145). For example, though Aka women have become members of the Village *Panchayats,* their status has not changed in the family and society. A social environment is needed to remove the contradiction between the legal and social realities and that is a slow process.

Table 3.2

Women Members in the Traditional Council

Tribe	*Only Men*	*Men and Some Women*	*I do Not Know*	*No Village Council*	*Total*
AKA					
Male	0	0	0	53	53
Female	0	0	0	47	47
M + F	0	0	0	100	100
ADIBASI					
Male	0	0	1	33	34
Female	0	0	6	60	66
M + F	0	0	7	93	100
ANGAMI					
Male	6	47	0	0	53
Female	4	43	0	0	47
M + F	10	90	0	0	100
DIMASA					
Male	54	0	0	0	54
Female	46	0	0	0	46
M + F	100	0	0	0	100
GARO					
Male	36	14	0	0	50
Female	41	9	0	0	50
M + F	77	23	0	0	100
Grand Total	187	113	7	193	500

Thus, change has not been uniform and not all of it favours gender equity. A positive change is the near disappearance of discrimination in primary education. 492 out of 500 respondents supported the idea of female literacy but not all were ready to send girls for higher education. The Garo and Angami have made great strides in women's higher education but the remaining tribes do not seem to be ready for it. Reasons for it are not hard to find. The Aka and the Dimasa are close to their tradition that assigns a higher status to men. Only recently, they have gained access to schools. The step is too big for *Adibasi* women who are at this stage trying to put up with prevailing impoverishment. Whatever money they and the remaining tribes have, has to be spent judiciously and they tend to invest it on boys whom they perceive as the future of the family (Vanlalchhawna, 2006: 71-74).

There is ambiguity also on the issue of women taking up salaried jobs. In the 500 families studied, 285 of 800 female members above 20 years of age are employed in the formal sector but it is not uniform among all. Only two Aka women have salaried jobs against 24 men. *Adibasi* women get wages as tea garden workers. Only seven of their men and three women have other jobs. On the other hand, 46 per cent of Garo and 31 per cent of Angami women above 20 years have salaried jobs against 14 out of 129 Dimasa women. It also means that education does not push women automatically into a salaried job. Their educational opportunities are limited, and where they exist, there may be hidden discrimination against them in employment because of the perception of men as breadwinners. That explains why only a third of the respondents supported the idea of women taking up salaried jobs. Besides, a third of those who supported it, perceived women's employment only as an additional source of income. They were not concerned about equality.

Demand to Return to the Customary Laws

That is the context of the demand to return to the customary law. There are several issues involved in it. Most respondents consider a return to the customary law basic to their identity and culture. However, very few are aware of the issues around it. There is firstly, a conservative "going back" that can take the tribe back to the past without gender justice. More often than not, it is a reinterpretation of the law more in favour of men than in the past. As the Angami experience shows, it can happen even when women demand equality. Thus, there is much ambiguity in such an interpretation. Some others want the tribe to go back to the past with no change. Such an approach as well as the type of reinterpretation is bound to go against women.

The second demand is for the codification of the customary law.

There are several risks in it, the first being the danger of the policy makers imposing a single law and thus going against tribal diversity. The relationship of the local to the national is as problematic today as it was five decades ago when many personal laws were changed (The Telegraph, 2005) mainly because many decision-makers perceive national unity as derived from New Delhi. For five decades, integration has more often than not come from the top to the detriment of the local knowledge, customs and cultural practices. Such a codification can result in stagnation. For example, the Mizo are the only tribe of the North East to have codified its customary law. When the need to revise them arose, they had to go through the process of codification once again in order to introduce them. The village councils and other male-dominated systems controlled this process. Largely, they do not favour women. Codification thus imposes the culture of a formal law on the living tradition of a customary law (Vitso, 2003).

The main issue is the patriarchal ethos of the customary law that ignores gender justice. If the laws are codified, they will formalise this culture of inequality and women will have very little power to change it. Instead, their laws have to be changed to suit this need and that requires a grass roots level process. If the official agencies are ready to respect their identity, there is a strong case for granting statutory recognition to the customary laws in order to bridge the gap between the national and the local. However, that raises the issue of territory. In their tradition, each tribe is linked to a territory. Much of tribal history is replete with the heroics of men who defended their territory against other tribes or from invaders from outside. However, today very few regions have a single tribe in a territory but the Sixth Schedule as well as recognition of the customary law link a territory to one tribe.

That lays the foundation of ethnic conflicts, as the Bihari-Karbi tension in Karbi Anglong and other ethnic conflicts in the region show. Tripura is another example of outsiders encroaching on tribal land and their communities trying to defend their territory (Bhaumik, 2003: 84-85). In addition, other conflicts like Kuki-Naga, Boro-Santhal and Dimasa-Hmar need to be studied in this context. One has to learn from these events and base recognition of the customary law on the reality of a separation between a tribe from its territory. One possibility is to separate the territory from the customary law. A tribe may be allowed to run its affairs according to its customary law but it would be personal jurisdiction that is not extended to a territory. Its members would come under its customary law wherever they live. That would protect its land and identity without causing ethnic conflicts.

This compromise cannot be imposed from above but has to be achieved through a serious reflection among the leaders on their customary laws. For it to be effective, the policy makers should begin by accepting the importance of the customary laws for their culture and identity search. Refusal to understand this basic need of the tribes can go against serious reflection. Their customary law needs to be recognised also in order to prevent encroachment of their land by outsiders. Many tribes in the region run their affairs according to this law but in the absence of its legal recognition, outsiders can deprive them of their livelihood with impunity. Land is central to their customary law and identity and it should be accorded legal protection (Fernandes and Bharali, 2006: 109-111). Separation of the territory from the tribe requires a major change in jurisprudence. It has to be understood more according to the Christian, Hindu and Muslim personal laws than as customary laws linked to a territory.

However, one cannot stop at the recognition of the land rights of a tribe and of the customary law around it. The law needs to be modified to suit the imperatives of gender justice. That can be done through conditional recognition of their law to suit the principle of class and gender equity. It involves recognition of the law as a whole but not of each one of its clauses. Some changes like women's representation in their political bodies may even have to be imposed as a condition for its recognition but much of it will have to come through a process of reflection with the tribe. Thus, recognition of the tribal customary law is to be based not on a conservative past or centralised nationalism but on their diversity, identity and the democratic value of equality of classes and sexes.

It also involves recognition of their community. One of the causes of the breakup of their communities is encouragement given to individual male owners to cultivate commercial crops. In addition, the approach of the administration can have the same effect. For example, the Integrated Tribal Development Programme (ITDP) is purely individual-based. It gives subsidies and loans to individual members of the tribe. That can result in class formation and strengthening of patriarchy since a few individuals can monopolise it. It is important to give schemes like ITDP to the whole village, not to individuals (Roy Burman, 1993: 182-183).

Education is another area of individualism and nationalism negating their diversity. The social, cultural and political systems as well as the history taught to them belong to "mainland" India. For example, a child studying at Dimapur in Nagaland knows all about the Junagadh or Jhansi Fort but nothing about the Dimasa fort just outside the town. Education needs to focus on the community and combine their identity with national unity. One cannot ignore education because that has been a major factor in awareness building on equality among the tribes in general and tribal women in particular. However, one cannot turn unity into uniformity. One has to adapt the system to their identity needs and that requires major changes in the syllabus of the North East (Singh, 2004: 115-119).

Moreover, legal changes cannot be effective without creating a social environment in their favour. For example, the Aka have banned child marriage but its vestiges remain in the form of women in their teens being forced into marriage. Early marriage adds to their subordination. The *Panchayat* should be mandated to ensure free consent and late marriage. It also shows the need to focus on education, for example, to stop child labour and emigration of *Adivasi* girl children as domestic helps. In introducing these changes, one can learn from the Angami among whom many women have some positive benefits of modernisation and have experienced a political process that helped them to become aware of their rights. However, its positive effects are wearing off because of competition for land and jobs. Relatively few younger men have internalised the political fervour of the struggle. As a result, the patriarchal ethos is taking over once again, particularly in their traditional political systems and women's inheritance rights. The Constitution was amended to recognise their customary law. Angami women only need its modernisation, not a return to the past (Fernandes and Barbora, 2002: 90-92):

In some cases, it may be important not to introduce the change. For example, some Garo men want male inheritance but are not ready to share social and political power with women. There is a strong case in such a situation to demand gender equality, not women's rights alone. Women from some other tribes demand equality with men but men in matrilineal tribes want inheritance without sharing social power. What is needed is gender equality in which men share social power with women in exchange for a share in inheritance. Most women, who demand inheritance, speak of gender equality, not of exclusive control. Such equality extending to political rights can add to their equity-based identity.

Conclusion

This chapter has discussed the interface of customary laws with modern inputs and its impact on women's status among five tribes that have felt its impact at various levels. Modernisation has facilitated changes in the tribes, some of them positive, others negative. Education has been the main catalyst of change along with factors like the formal administrative and political systems and change of religion. Some changes in their customary law and institutions that have resulted from these inputs favour women's rights while others go against them. Besides, some men have started reinterpreting their customary law to suit their own needs. Despite education, some tribes do not support women's equal access to jobs. On the other side, inputs like education and the SHGs have been helping some women to become aware of their right to equality. The benefits of modernisation change according to the tribe. The Angami men as well as women have many benefits while the *Adivasi* have felt its worst effects.

However, even the benefits, at times, go hand in hand with the trend to strengthen the patriarchal ethos. As women become aware of their rights, also resistance to their aspirations can grow. That is the context of the demand for the recognition of their customary law that is intrinsic to tribal identity. As such, it has to be recognised. However, while doing so, national unity interpreted as uniformity should not get priority. A balance has to be struck between unity and diversity. Besides, the customary law should not be identified with a tribe's territory. Moreover, one cannot accept or reject the customary law with no changes. One has to recognise its totality but not every clause. It has to be changed from the perspective of gender and class equity.

These challenges have to be faced while accepting the customary law as intrinsic to tribal identity. A debate has to be encouraged to create a climate of reflection in order to encourage them to face the challenge of finding an identity based on the norms of class and gender equity and the imperatives of dealing with the present day world. That is another type of modernisation.

References

Banu, Z. 2001. *Tribal Women Empowerment and Gender Issues.* New Delhi: Kanishka Publishers.

Barbora, S. 2002. 'Ethnic politics and land use: Genesis of Conflicts in India's North-East', *Economic and Political Weekly,* 37:1[illegible]5-1292.

Barpujari, S.K. 1997. *History of the Dimasas.* North Cachar Hills: District Autonomous Council.

Bhaumick, S. 2003. 'Tripura's Gumti dam must go', *The Ecologist Asia* 11: 84-89.

Bordoloi, B.N. 1984. *The Dimasa Kacharis of Assam.* Guwahati: Tribal Research Institute.

D'Souza, A. and C. Kekrieseno. 2002. *Coping with Social Change in North-East India. A Comparative Study of Three Ethnic Groups in North-East India-Aka, Angami and Dimasa.* Jakhama: St. Joseph's College.

D'Souza, A. 2005. *Traditional Systems of Forest Conservation in North East India: The Angami Tribe of Nagaland.* Guwahati: North Eastern Social Research Centre.

Fernandes, W. and G. Bharali. 2006. *Development-Induced Displacement in Assam 1947-2000: A Quantitative and Qualitative Study of its Extent and Nature. (Mimeo),* Guwahati: North Eastern Social Research Centre.

Fernandes, W. and M. Pereira. 2005. *Land Relations and Ethnic Conflicts: The Case of Northeast India.* Guwahati: North Eastern Social Research Centre.

Fernandes, W. and S. Barbora. 2002. *Modernisation and Women's Status in North Eastern India: A Comparative Study of Six Tribes.* Guwahati: North Eastern Social Research Centre.

Fernandes, W.; M. Pereira and V. Khatso. 2005. *Customary Laws in North East India: Impact on Women.* (mimeo), Guwahati: North Eastern Social Research Centre.

Goswami, M.C. 1982. *Customary Laws and Practices of the Garo of Meghalaya.* Guwahati: Law Research Institute.

Goswami, M.C.1985. *The Customary Laws and Practices of the Angami Nagas of Nagaland.* Guwahati: Law Research Institute.

Goswami, M.C. 1986. *The Customary Laws of the Dimasa of Assam.* Guwahati: Law Research Institute.

Marak, C. 1997. 'Status of women in Garo culture'. In Soumen Sen (Ed): *Women in Meghalaya.* pp. 56-72. New Delhi: Omsons Publications.

Menon, G. 1995. 'The impact of migration on the work and tribal women's status'. In Loes Schenken-Sandbergen (Ed): *Women and Seasonal Labour Migration.* pp. 79-154. New Delhi: Sage Publications.

Nongbri, T. 1998. 'Gender issues and tribal development'. In Bhupinder Singh (Ed). *Antiquity to Modernity,* Vol. II, *Tribal Self-Management in Northeast India,* pp. 221-246. New Delhi: Inter India Publications.

Roy Burman, B. K. 1993. 'Tribal population: Interface of historical ecology and political economy'. In Mrinal Miri (Ed): *Continuity and Change in Tribal Society.* pp. 175-216. Shimla: Indian Institute of Advanced Study.

Ruivah, K., 2002, 'Christianity and social change among the Tangkhuls of Manipur'. In S. M. Channa (Ed). *The Christian Mission: Christianity and Tribal Religion,* pp. 123-140. New Delhi: Cosmo Publications.

Sanyu, V. 1996. *A History of Nagas and Nagaland: Dynamics of Traditional Village Formation.* New Delhi: Commonwealth Publishers.

Sharma, J.L. and R.K. Kar. 1993. 'Continuity and change among the migrant Oraons: A case study in Assam'. In Mrinal Miri (Ed): *Continuity and Change in Tribal Society,* pp. 129-141. Shimla: Indian Institute of Advanced Study.

Singh, J. P. 2004. 'School education in Northeast India: Issues and prospects'. In Biloris Lyndem and Utpal Kumar De (Eds): *Education in North East India: Experiences and Challenges,* pp. 99-122. New Delhi: Concept Publishing Company.

Sinha, R. 1962. *The Akas.* Itanagar: Directorate of Research, North Eastern Frontier Agency.

The Telegraph. 2005. 'Who's integration?' Editorial, *The Telegraph,* 3rd September.

Vanlalchawna. 2006. *Higher Education in North-East India.* New Delhi: Mittal Publications.

Vitso, A. 2003. *Customary Law and Women. The Chakhesang Nagas,* New Delhi: Regency Publications.

Zehol, L. 1998. 'The Tangkhul women today'. In Lucy Zehol (Ed): *Women in Naga Society,* pp. 20-29. New Delhi: Regency Publications.

4 Identity Construction Through Fission: The Case of the Desi, Paliya and Rajbansi Paliya of Southern North Bengal

Rajatsubhra Mukhopadhyay

I

Like ethnicity, caste in India is not a fixed and rigid form of identification. Out of various socio-economic and political reasons, certain castes have changed their 'ascribed' and 'cultural' identity through several processes. The modes of identity construction in the case of castes in India are therefore an area of considerable interest among the sociologists and social anthropologists engaged in caste studies. Particularly from the point of view of processes involved in the formation and transformation of caste in India, such an understanding was necessary both from academic and policy perspectives, and thus, occupied an important place in the colonial and post-colonial ethnography (Bayly, 1997, 2000; Dirks, 2008).

Redefinition of cultural boundaries is historically used to help raise caste rank or social mobility. The quest for spiritual improvement has often led to the usual quest for higher rank. Once a new caste or a sub-caste is formed through any of these processes of redefinition and regrouping, it maintains its own cultural distinctiveness and group identity as other castes do in the same territory.

The segmentation within a caste normally took place when a part/ section of it inclined to adopt a reference model different from that held by the rest of the group. The member of this section sanskritise their customs and rituals with an aim to achieve a higher status than their parent body. Hutton (1980) draws our attention to the fissiparous tendencies of castes where a kind of tendency has been noticed among certain castes to split-up and throw off fresh endogamous unit molded with new social identity. This phenomenon according to Hutton persisted from very early times and historically led to the formation of 'sub-castes'. He has written quite extensively on the process of segregation, separation and fission of castes in India. In this process of new identity construction in caste society through fission and other modes, it was the census bureaucracy of British India that ultimately decided which sub-castes should be recorded independently, and which are to be clubbed together. That often led to considerable confusion over identity question of different castes and 'sub-castes' in India.

On identity issue of castes, Heredia observes that both caste and ethnic communities have multiple group histories and oral tradition, folk tales and folklore to sustain and perpetuate their distinctiveness, whether cultural or sub-cultural. Thus, both ethnicity and caste are socially constructed, but they also have a foundation in the material history and circumstances of the community (2000: 45 and 49). Heredia's observations appear quite relevant in addressing the problem of internal structure of different castes or their sub-groups. Taking this point into consideration, the present chapter aims to explore the case of Desi, Paliya, and Rajbansi Paliya castes of southern North Bengal, as they still suffer from some kind of disputed, ill-defined and confusing identity. In advancing the arguments, insights have been drawn from some earlier ethnographic accounts of the castes under consideration and are mostly found in Malda, North Dinajpur and South Dinajpur districts of West Bengal.

II

Numerically and ethnically, the Desi, Paliya and Rajbansi Paliya occupy an important place in the southern districts of North Bengal which include Malda and two (south and north) Dinajpur districts. Geographically, they have greater concentration in the region between river Kulik and river Tangan, an area stretching over the south and parts of north Dinajpur district. They also have a sizable population in the Malda district Despite their greater representation in the local population, their origin and social history is still obscure, and their ethnic identity appears somewhat confusing and controversial.Their existing history is largely based on the accounts left by the colonial administrators and ethnographers. Afterwards, there has been hardly any attempt to locate their exact ethnic identity and affinity. Practically, there is no anthropological or sociological study on their social formation and identity construction. The ethnographic accounts, whatever little is available on them, are highly speculative and hardly offer any clear cut idea about the position of the caste, sub-castes and groups in the local hierarchy. Their social history is so obscured that one may get confused while studying and ranking them as a distinct caste. For example, in the *Handbook of Scheduled Castes and Scheduled Tribes of West Bengal,* published by the Government of West Bengal in 1966, and particularly on the question of social position of the Paliyas, it has been categorically mentioned, "Details as to the social status of the Paliyas are not available" (Das *et al.,* 1966: 87).

On the question of ethnic affinity of the *Desis,* the available ethnographies offer diverse views. In the first instance, it is generally admitted that the Desi/ Desiya/ Desi Rajbansi/ Debasarma are not distinct castes. They are mere sub-divisions of the original Koch or Paliya caste. It is often said, in the Malda region, the Debasarmas are not perfect Hindus from the standpoint of their origin. The Desis are locally recognised as the descendent of those Koches who were the early settlers of this clime. The very nomenclature of *desi* has probably originated from the Bengali term *desh* which literally means the countrymen.

The Desis mostly call them as Debasarma. They trace their mythical origin from Brahmans, and of late, have begun to wear the sacred thread to justify the claim of their twice-born (Brahmanic) status. An educated section of the Desis has taken up its surname as Sarkar.

The Desis identify themselves as the original inhabitants of the region. They are strongly inclined to represent themselves as a distinct caste and completely separated from the Paliya, Rajbansi and others (Mukhopadhyay, 1964: 236). The census authorities, however, do not agree with this view and the Desis are not enumerated separately. The census of West Bengal has recognised the Paliya, Rajbansi and Koch as three separate Scheduled Castes but not the Desis. It is interesting to note that, in villages of South Dinajpur district, the Desis prefer to call them 'Desi Rajbansi' and do not hesitate to include them in the census category of caste as 'Rajbansi'. According to their explanation, there are four sub-castes among the Rajbansis. They are namely—Kshatriya

Rajbansi, Desi Rajbansi (Desiya), Paliya Rajbansi (Paliya) and Koch-Kantai Rajbansi (Rajbansi Paliya). Based on this classification, the Desis enjoy the status of Scheduled Caste as assigned to the 'Rajbansis' in general. The fusion of the Desis with the generic category of 'Rajbansi' is perhaps of a recent origin. Since castes in Bengal became self-conscious, to which the recording of castes in the census was made in order of precedence that contributed a great deal. In this process of enumeration, no one wanted to remain a Sudra. Thus, unlike many other castes including the Paliyas who asked for Kshatriya status (Mitra, 1953: 22), the Desiyas claimed for a Brahmin status.

The Desis still regard themselves as socially and ritually superior to the Paliyas. Long back, Risley (1998: 493) noted that a Desi can take rice, water, sweet meet, etc., from a Paliya man, but not from a Paliya woman, nor is there any practice of intermarriage between the two groups. The Desis claim, of having superior status compared to the Paliyas, had been legitimatised with an argument that they do not plough with cows or use them to turn oil mills (*ghani*).

According to Risley, the Desiya may be the modern representative of *desi*, a sort of rudimentary priest earlier found among the Pani-Koch. He further claims that the construction of new Desi identity clearly reflects the method how tribes which adopt Hinduism tend continually to get rid of their pre-Hindu pattern of grouping and to remodel their internal structures in the tune of orthodox Hindu way of life (Risley, 1998: 493-94).

In the villages, the Desiyas claimed to be superior in the social scale as compared to the Paliyas. So, they conform more strictly to Hindu customs. They began wearing sacred thread with a claim that originally they were Brahmins. To establish their claim, they invited Brahmins from Banaras for a favourable judgment, and similarly official measures from the court were also taken to declare themselves as 'Debasarma' and not 'Desiya' any more (Mukhopadhyay, 1964: 240-41). They wanted to elevate them in the local caste hierarchy by adopting many Brahmanic norms and practices. By their strict adherence to endogamy and other orthodox Hindu manners and customs, the Desiya prefer to identify them as a distinct caste separated from the Paliyas and Rajbansis. In the rural belts of South Dinajpur, the Desiyas represent the picture of a different community though they are little known to the government officials and sociologists/ anthropologists. In parts of Malda district, they designate them as 'Gour Desis', i.e., an inhabitants of erstwhile Gour, the capital of famous Pal, and afterwards, the Sen Dynasties of Bengal.

III

There is practically no literature which fully describes the origin, migration history and socio-economic life of the Paliya. Local people speculate that the term *Paliya* is nothing but a Bengali conversion of *paliye* (flee), and which means the Paliyas had fled from a different place and later settled in this parts of Bengal. Risley noted that Paliya is said by some to refer to the flight (*palayan*) of the supposed Kshatriya ancestors of the tribe. He apprehends that it is equally possible that the name Paliya is merely a variant of the first half of the name Pani-Koch by which they started designating themselves as Paliya at the beginning of the 20th century (Risley, 1998: 492). Risley was of view that Paliya, Poli, Pola are Dravidian castes of North Bengal. They were originally Koch by ethnic affinity, and among whom, there are grounds for suspecting some admixture of Mongoloid blood.

The Poli or Paliya, an off-shoot of the Koch tribe, are by far the most numerous castes in both North and South Dinajpur districts. Like many other castes of aboriginal descent, they claim to be Kshatriyas. They assert their appellation of *Poli* (means to flee in Bengali) is derived from their ancestors having fled from the wrath of Parasurama, the Brahmin warrior incarnation of Vishnu, in his war of extermination against the Kshatriyas.

The Eastern Bengal District Gazetteers: Dinajpur (Strong, 1912) described the Paliya as a semi-Hinduised caste. The Government enlisted them as a separate Scheduled Caste distinct from the Rajbansis. Even then, a section of Paliyas still prefer to call them Rajbansi. They said that Paliya and Rajbansi are practically convertible terms. It has been pointed out by Balle in 1942 that the Rajbansi-Kshatriyas, who are now found in the districts of Rangpur, Jalpaiguri and Cooch Behar in large numbers, were formerly known as Paliya (Chattopadhyay, 2002: 573-74).

The Paliyas are divided into two endogamous groups. They are namely, the *Sadhu* or *Bhajana* Paliya and the *Babahari* or *Babu* Paliya. Few scholars prefer to list *Desi* Paliya (discussed above as Desi or Desiya) as the third off-shoot of the main Paliya stock. The basic distinction between the Sadhu and Babu Paliya lies in the fact that the latter indulge in wine and animal food while these food items are forbidden to the Sadhu Paliya. The Babu Paliyas are akin to the Rajbansis in manners and customs. The Sadhu Paliyas are mostly the followers of Chaitanya and claimed to be Kshatriyas by Varna. Many of them have taken sacred-thread and follow the manners of high caste Hindus. There are no commensal and connubial relations between the Sadhu and Babu Paliyas. According to Majumdar, it is highly probable if not certain that the Paliyas, Babu Paliyas and Rajbansis are of the same extraction and are now precipitating into different communities due to cultural disintegration (Majumdar, 1926: 168). That observation of Majumdar is quite revealing with reference to the question of formation and identity construction of castes through the modes of fission.

IV

The Kontai-Koches are another small group found scattered in distribution in parts of South Dinajpur district. The earlier Koches of this district were *palki* (palanquin) bearer by profession. At that time their surname was *kaisya* or *kahar*. Since the time of discarding that occupation they have been using the surname 'Rajbansi' and should not be confused with the general Rajbansi population of northern Bengal, and particularly that of the Cooch Behar and Jalpaiguri districts.

There is reason to believe that the local people with the 'Rajbansi' title were belonging to the *Kontai* section of the Koches. This particular section of people does not consider themselves connected either to the Paliya or to the Desiya. Normally, they are not served by the priests of the latter two communities.

Long back Simha noted that all the Koches of the undivided Dinajpur district originally belonged to the Dalai sub-caste/section of the Koches though they themselves do not know it (1902: 21). The Desis are so called because they were palanquin bearers, from *dola* a *palki*, and in that they differ from the Paliya and the Desiya. Intermarriage among them is also forbidden. The Dalai, according to

Buchanan (1838), are a fishing group whose pursuit is fishing in the shallow drains or ditches. The poorer section of this community still follows many of their traditional manners and customs and is indifferently called Rajbansi, Koch or Rajbansi Paliya. So, they are often confused with the general Rajbansi population of North Bengal. Their number also reduced by 1941 as at the time of enumeration they were clubbed with the Rajbansis in general.

V

From several ethnographic accounts, it appears that the castes namely Desi, Paliya, Koch and Rajbansi have originated from a common stock and this seems to be admitted generally. Risley (1998) mentioned that the Koches have ten-sub castes including the above mentioned ones and their sub-groups. Most of these sub-castes have been formed by change in their custom. The immediate case of this type of formation is the Paliya and its division into 'Sadhu' and 'Babu' categories. As a general explanation, the main distinction between the Babu and Sadhu Paliyas lies in the fact that while the former indulge in strong drinks and animal food, it is forbidden to the latter. In fact, the Paliyas bearing similar name are the product of fission of an original stock. In the case of Paliya, each sub-division is again divided into smaller regional endogamous sections distributed over several villages in the territory.

VI

There is every reason to believe that, ethnically, the Desi, Paliya, Rajbansi and Koch have a common origin. The Rajbansis of North Bengal, however, emphatically deny any affinity between the original Rajbansis and the Desi, Paliya and Kontai-Koches. A closer study of the so called sub-castes within the major groups reveals the fact that they are the product of fission. At some point, the basis of this distinction was purely territorial. For instance, a section of Desi/Desiyas in Malda district prefer to get designated the as 'Gour Desi', while their customs and habits are quite akin to the other Desis of the region.

During the colonial period, the process of fission was more pronounced where many aspirant castes and sub-castes started changing their old cultural practices in order to attain superior status in the caste hierarchy. The perpetual division and segmentation among the earlier Koches is a clear reflection of this type of social formation through fission. Such fission was intimately associated with some kind of cultural mobility among some low ranking castes, and sub-castes possibly originated from a common ethnic stock. This particular form of fission normally took place when a section of a caste desired to adopt a reference model which was quite different from their original one. As a case in point, one may refer to the fission of Paliyas into two sub-castes namely Babu/Desi Paliya and Sadhu Paliya purely in cultural terms. In that split, the Sadhu Paliyas sanskritised their manners and customs with an aim to achieve a relatively superior status in the local caste hierarchy. In early part of the twentieth century, many of them were accommodated in certain generic categories for administrative reason. For instance, the Desis and Koches, isolated local castes of Malda, were bracketed with all Bengal Rajbansi caste in the census (Roy, 1984: 69). However, some other castes which found them mentioned in the census, in many places, again got divided internally into exclusive endogamous and commensal units. They, from all practical considerations, preferred to get identified and function as sub-castes. Among them, sanctions were extended to maintain the rules of both internal and external behaviour.

Redefinition of cultural boundaries thus helped in social mobility and in forming new sub-castes. They started to follow a distinct rule about their commensal and connubial relations with other castes and sub-castes. Some members of a lower caste group adopted means to change of their occupation and to get separated from their former fellow caste men. For instance, the members of Kontai/Dalai Koches referred them with the surname 'Rajbansi', since having discarded the occupation of palanquin bearer. The fission of castes through occupational change was noted by British ethnographers of the nineteenth century. That particular phenomenon continued to get mentioned even in their ethnographic reports published in the later period. During British Raj, the fission of castes was a regular phenomenon. Out of this process, several sub-castes were formed mainly by separating themselves from their original stock. And that helped them in ensuring social mobility. Some kind of cultural drift added to this process of schism, and the off-shoots of certain castes/tribes eventually became wholly separated.

Mayer draws our attention to the social unit which he calls the 'sub-caste' defined as the "smallest endogamous unit" within a caste (Mayer, 1986: 91). His observation appears quite valid when we see the Desiya/Debasarma do not marry the *Choto-Desiya*, a sub-section of the Debasarmas, and who are considered to be inferior in social ranking. Similarly, the connubial relations between Sadhu and Babu Paliyas are strictly prohibited. All these sub-castes thus follow the rule of endogamy to present themselves as a distinct caste/sub-caste though ethnically they have a common origin. The process of segregation, separation and fission of castes, thus, institutionalised through the practice of endogamy. Moreover, this unequal status of two groups within the same nomenclature often makes it difficult to ascertain that their social status hailed from the two adjoining districts located well within same region as we observed in the case of southern North Bengal.

VII

Since late 19th century, a kind of fissiparous tendency has been noticed among several castes (mostly middle and low ranked) and tribes aspirant for social mobility. Among the available modes of social mobility, the fission of caste was one of the preferred models. So, the method of construction of caste identity through fission has attracted the attention of some scholars. This phenomenon is worth investigating since caste has been a tenacious and persistent signifier of identity in India (Betteile, 2012).

In the present chapter, an attempt has been made to examine the mode of identity construction through fission as observed in the castes of the Desi, Paliya and Rajbansi Paliya. These castes are mostly found in the three southern districts (namely Malda, North Dinajpur and South Dinajpur) of northern Bengal. Mainly based on ethnographic accounts (though scanty), the chapter intends to look into the case of the above mentioned castes as they still suffer from some kind of controversial and confusing identity. So far, there has been hardly any attempt to locate their ethnic identity and affinity anthropologically or sociologically. Though, they ethnically and numerically occupy an important place in the ethnic map of southern North Bengal, their origin and social history is still obscure and their identity is somewhat puzzling.

It is generally admitted that the Desi/Desiya/Desi Rajbansi/ Debasarma are not distinct castes. They are mere sub-divisions of the original Koch or Paliya caste. The Desis mostly designate them as

Debasarma and trace their mythological origin from Brahmans. They, thus, wear the sacred thread and conform more strictly to the Hindu customs to justify their twice-born status. They identify themselves as the original inhabitants of the region. The census authorities, however, do not agree with this view and socially bracket them with the Rajbansi. So, they equally enjoy the status of Scheduled Castes in West Bengal. But in the villages, the Desiyas prefer to identify them as a distinct caste separated from both the Paliya and Rajbansi.

The Poli or Paliya is by far the most numerous castes in both North and South Dinajpur districts. They claimed to be Kshatriya and their very application of *Poli* (means flee) is derived from their ancestors having fled from the wrath of Parasurama in his war of extremation against the Kshatriya. The British officials were of view that 'Paliya' and 'Rajbansi' are practically converted terms. They felt that the Rajbansi-Kshatriyas, who are now found in the districts of Jalpaiguri, Cooch Behar and Rangpur (now in Bangladesh) in numerous numbers, were formerly known as Paliya.

The Paliyas are further divided into two sub-castes, namely, Sadhu or pure Paliya and Babu Paliya mainly based on their culinary habit. It is highly probable, if not certain, that Sadhu Paliyas, Babu Paliyas and Rajbansis are of the same extraction and are now precipitating into different communities due to fission and cultural disintegration. The Sadhu Paliya claimed to be Kshatriyas by Varna, take the sacred-thread and follow the manners of high caste Hindus. The Babu Paliyas, on the other hand, are akin to the Rajbansis in their manners and customs. There is no commensal and connubial relation between the Babu and Sadhu Paliyas.

Another small and ethnically distinct group, called Kontai-Koches, are found in disperses in parts of South Dinajpur district. It is interesting to note that since the time of discarding their traditional calling of palanquin *(palki)* bearer, they have been using the surname 'Rajbansi', and therefore, should not be confused with the general and greater Rajbansi population of North Bengal. In the villages, they are indifferently called Rajbansi Koch or Rajbansi Paliya. They do not consider themselves connected either to the Paliyas or to the Desiyas. A large number of them still follow many of their pre-Hinduised manners and customs. Their number also reduced by 1941 census as at the time of enumeration they were clubbed with the Rajbansis, in general.

During the colonial period, the process of fission of castes/tribes was more pronounced as many aspirant castes and sub-castes stove their old cultural practices in order to attain a superior status in the local caste hierarchy. The perpetual segmentation among the earlier tribal Koches is a clear reflection of identity construction through fission. That mode was intimately associated with some kind of social mobility through cultural change and adoption of a reference model quite alien to them and their original culture. They, from all practical considerations, preferred to identify and function as a 'sub-caste'. They also started to follow a distinct rule in the matter of their commensal and connubial relations with other castes and sub-castes. Some kind of cultural drift added to this process of schism and the off shoots of certain castes/tribes eventually got separated. This fission of castes ultimately institutionalised through the practice of endogamy, as we observed in the case of the Desi, Paliya and Kontai/Rajbansi Paliya of southern North Bengal, despite the fact that possibly they have a common origin in terms of ethnic affinity.

References

Bayly, Susan. 1997. 'Caste and race in the colonial ethnography of India'. In Peter Robb (Ed): *The Concept of Race in South Asia*, pp. 165 – 217, Delhi: Oxford University Press.

Bayly, Susan. 2000. *Caste, Society and Politics: From the Eighteenth Century to Modern Age*, pp. 165 – 217, Cambridge University Press.

Beteille, Andre. 2012. 'The peculiar tenacity of caste', *The Economic and Political Weekly*, 47, 13: 41-48.

Buchanan, Francis. 1838. 'Accounts of Rangpur (Rangapura)'. In R. Montgomery Martin (Ed): *The History, Antiquities, Topography and Statistics of Eastern India*, London: W.H. Allen.

Chattopadhyaya, Annapurna. 2002. *The People and Culture of Bengal: A Study of Origin* (Vol. I, Part 2*)*, Calcutta: Firma KLM Pvt. Ltd.

Das, Amal Kumar, Bidyut Kumar Roy Chowdhury and Manish Kumar Raha. 1966. *Handbook on Scheduled Castes and Scheduled Tribes in West Bengal* (Bulletin of the Cultural Research Institute, Special Series – 8), Calcutta: Government of West Bengal (Tribal Welfare Dept.).

Dirks, Nicholas B. 2008. *Castes of Mind: Colonialism and the Making of Modern India*, Delhi: Permanent Black.

Heredia, Rudolf C. 2000. 'Subaltern alternatives on caste, class and ethnicity', *Contributions to Indian Sociology*, 34, 1: 37 – 62.

Hutton, J.H. 1980. *Caste in India: Its Nature, Function, and Origin*, Bombay: Oxford University Press.

Majumdar, D.N. 1926. 'Pseudo Rajputs: The Polias, Palias, Babu Polias or Rajbansis of North Bengal: An instance of the formation of tribes into castes', *Man in India*, 6: 155 – 173.

Mayer, Adrian C. 1986. *Caste and Kinship in Central India: A Village and its Region*, London: Routledge and Kegan Paul.

Mitra, A. 1953. *Census of India 1951, West Bengal: The Tribes and Castes of West Bengal*, Calcutta: West Bengal Government Press.

Mukhopadyay, Tarasish. 1964. 'A note on the Debasarmas of West Dinajpur', *Man in India*, 44, 3: 233 – 246.

Risley, H.H. 1998. *Tribes and Castes of Bengal: Ethnographic Glossary*, Vol. I, Calcutta: Firma KLM Pvt. Ltd.

Roy, Rajat Kanta. 1984. *Social Conflict and Political Unrest in Bengal 1875 - 1927*, Delhi: Oxford University Press.

Simha, Hari Mohan. 1902. 'Notes on the Koch, Paliya, and the Rajvanci in Dinajpur', *Journal of the Asiatic Society of Bengal*, 31, 3: 20-25.

Strong, F.W. 1912. *Eastern Bengal District Gazetteers: Dinajpur* (Reprint), Siliguri: N.L. Publishers.

5 Socio-political Dimensions of Ethnic Movement in Assam

Girin Phukon

Mobilisation of people on ethnic line has been a dominant feature of the politics of North East India. Ever since the independence of the country, the North East India has been passing through a crisis leading to ethnic movement. The insurgent activities of a section of the Nagas, Mizos (presently petered out), Tripura Tribals, Meities of Manipur; the ethnic assertion of the Karbis, Khasis, Garo and Arunachalis in the hills and the Bodo, Kacharis, Tiwas, Rabhas, Misings, Ahoms, Chutias, Deories, Koch Rajbonshis, Moran, Matak; of late, the Assam movement on the issue of infiltration in the plains are the manifestation of the urges and aspirations of these ethnic communities for their all round development. Use of cultural emblems of the ethnic group for socio-political and economic ends gives rise to ethnicity. In fact, ethnicity is a sense of ethnic awareness. Ethnic mobilisation is, however, conditioned by the overall political and economic environment. The State operates within the broad political-economic environment and therefore, its action is largely governed by the economic laws. As the laws of market economy give birth to uneven economic development, it widens the gaps between the ethnic groups living in different regions or sub-regions. It generates a sense of feeling of being relatively deprived among the ethnic groups of backward areas, which in turn precipitates political mobilisation on ethnic lines. Therefore, either ethnicity is the outward reaction of various socio-cultural groups against the existing politico-economic system wherein inequality or competition act as a catalyst in mobilising people based on ethnicity. It culminates into ethno-political movements demanding special constitutional safeguards of their respective identities, autonomous and separate States to secession. These ideas of articulation of ethnic interest are taken into account to understand the socio-political dynamics of ethnic movement in Assam.

This problem obviously led us to the question whether the movements launched by the ethnic groups would solve their basic problems. The present chapter is an endeavour to understand this question in the light of identity assertion of the ethnic groups in Assam.

II

Assam is a melting pot of diverse lingo-cultural ethnic groups. These groups may be broadly divided into two categories, viz., non-tribal and tribal ethnic groups. However, in the course of examining the problem, emphasis has been laid more on the latter. The tribal ethnic groups of Assam such as the Bodos, the Kacharis, the Karbis, the Mising, the Deuries, the Tiwas, the Rabhas and the non-tribal ethnic groups—the Ahoms, the Chutias, the Koch-Rajbonshis, and the Moran-Mattaks could not reap meaningful benefit from the British administration. As a result, these Mongoloid tribes became backward educationally, socially, economically, and even politically. The emerging educated elite of these groups, rightly or wrongly, began to feel that they being deprived of their 'due share' of administrative jobs and other privileges under the colonial rule. In view of this, some of the elites of these groups gradually felt the need of organising their respective communities on the basis of distinct lingo-cultural traits so as to remove their socio-economic backwardness which culminated in the formation of organisations like the Ahom Association (1893), the Koch Rajbonshi Sanmillan (1912), All Boro Chatra Sanmillan (1918), Kachari Sanmillan (1921), Boro Maha Sanmillan (1924), Moran-Matak Sanmillan (1937), and so on. These organisations put forward the demands such as adequate representation in the provincial Legislature, reservation of government jobs and seats in the educational institution, removal of social inequality, etc. In fact, the ethnic elites felt socially so neglected that in a memorandum submitted to the Simon Commission on September 14, 1928 at New Delhi, the Kachari Sanmillan complained that:

> Socially, the tribals are regarded as untouchables. To call them Hindus will be a misnomer in as much the Hindus do not accept them into their society, do not dine with them..... As the students of their community are not allowed to mess together with those of the Hindus, they naturally look for provision of separate messing in all the schools and colleges of Assam (Kachari Jubak Sanmilani, 1928; Deori, 1941).

Although the ethnic tribes were virtually absorbed into the Hindu social structure, they were accorded only low caste status in the Hindu social hierarchy. Indeed, it seemed them that they received a degraded position in the caste hierarchy of the Hindu dominated Assamese society. In effect, it led the plain tribals to feel that though they were the original inhabitants of the province, Assamese Hindu aristocracy had dispossessed them of their original rights.

III

Even after decades of independence of the country, the same feelings and sentiments continued among the ethnic tribes and races of Assam. They had not only been experiencing the problems of alienation, unemployment, economic and political oppression under the existing socio-political system but also discrimination in achieving their 'rightful' place in the society. In an undeveloped country like ours, economic development is accompanied by increased inequalities, because the rewards are allocated based on the strength and persistence of organised sector of society. In view of this, the ethnic groups of Assam began to organise their communities with new vigour. As a result, since the late sixties of the last century, the socio-cultural organisations such as the Bodo Sahitya Sabha, Mising Bane Kebang, Rabha Sahitya Sabha, Deuri Sahitya Sabha, Chutia Jati Sanmillan, Koch Rajbonshi Sanmillan, and the like, soon became articulate and began to revitalise the ethnic conciousness. The student wing of most of the ethnic groups such as All Boro Students' Union, Mising Students Union, Karbi Student Union, Sonowal-Kachari Student Union and many others became active in mobilising their respective communities. While examining the basic causes of identity consciousness and backwardness of the autochthon tribals, Gohain (1991) maintained:

> There has never been a sincere attempt on the part of the Assamese to uplift the tribal brethren on their level through reservation and other constitutional methods since the State machinery is dominated by the Assamese caste-Hindu, reservation in jobs and educational institutions has been sabotaged through neglect and obstructionism. In addition, what is worst, the areas reserved for them as tribal belts and blocks, there is no lack of evidence that this important safeguard has been hollow, to begin with, and has been made meaningless by the way, it has been encroached.

The obvious implication of the statement is that this factor had the potentiality of arousing ethnic movement in terms of distinct political boundary. In fact, social discrimination, caste-based Hindu social equation, and the superiority assumption of the caste Hindu dominated Assamese society were somehow responsible for pushing the tribals away from the greater Assamese society (Dutta, 1990). Obviously, therefore, most of the ethnic groups realised that the monopoly of political power of the dominant section of the Assamese was bound to restrict the scope of their aspirations and effort for development. Thus, a section of the emerging educated elite of the ethnic group began to feel that in order to establish their community into a rightful place; they must be politically powerful and assertive. For this purpose, some of them started forming certain political platforms such as – Plains Tribal Council of Assam, Ahom Tai Mongoloid Rajya Parishad (renamed as *Ujoni Asom Rajya Parishad*), Bodo People's Action Committee, United Tribal Nationalist Liberation Front, Karbi Autonomous State Demand Committee, Mising Autonomous State Demand Committee, Tiwa Autonomous State Demand Committee, Rabha Autonomous State Demand Committee, etc. It appears that, since late sixties, some of the ethnic groups became more articulate and organised and became capable of challenging the dominant position of the ruling Assamese elite and bargaining for adequate share of administrative jobs and political power (Phukon, 2003).

It may be reiterated, that in the beginning, the tribes and races started their assertion with non-political issues, i.e., protection of socio-cultural identity, development of their language, economic development, instruction through their mother tongue and so on. Subsequently, these culminated in political demands. The Official Language Bill of 1961 was perceived as a barrier to their advancement and as an obstacle to get jobs in the government offices. Soon after the passing of the Official Language Bill, the process of disintegration of the old Assam of the British days followed and Nagaland was made a separate State in 1963. The Medium Movement of 1972 further gave a fillip to this process and, as such, Meghalaya and Mizoram became separate from Assam in 1972 and 1986 respectively. The demand for separate and autonomous State in present Assam follows from this trend. Strange though it may seem, while the dominant Assamese elite wanted to protect themselves from the dominance of others, particularly the Bengalis, they at the sametime wanted to make the Assamese as the sole language of the multi-lingual State like Assam was in some way, similar to the idea of, enforcing the legitimacy of language of some of the ethnic groups being the language of their respective areas. Inspired by the identity consciousness of the Assamese, they have also become conscious of their distinct identity, have started reviving their language and projecting it as their symbol of identity to assert their rights through political mobilisation. The youth-student force of the ethnic groups appears to have been able to mobilise the people of their respective communities. Thus, it appears that the lingo-cultural and political movement for asserting Assamese identity led by the relatively advanced section of the Assamese has given birth to the ethnic movements in Assam.

The Assam movement (1979-1985) further sharpened the identity consciousness among the ethnic groups. This movement was perceived by most of the ethnic groups of Assam as a desperate attempt to consolidate the supremacy of Assamese Caste-Hindu middle class. The movement therefore triggered off various kinds of ethnic stir against this attempt, which have often acquired a kind of reactive chauvinism of their own (Gohain, 1991). Thus, the autochthon tribals have become restive against their 'oppressed statuses' in a high-caste dominated Assamese society and they have built up a massive movement following the Assam movement. The emerging ethnic leadership is not prepared to accept the hegemony of the upper caste dominated Assamese ruling class. This sentiment was articulated by Upendranath Brahma, the then President of All Bodo Student's Union (ABSU) while pleading for a separate Bodo State. Thus he maintained:

> The Assamese have no moral right to rule over the tribals of Assam—the sons of the soil. The Assamese are not original masters of Assam but they were actually intruders and salient aggressors who had unjustifiably snatched away the land of ours. The actual and original master of Assam is these deprived tribals—the Monglians. Mr. Prafulla Kumar Mahanta has no right to rule over the tribals nor can he claim not to divide Assam further because he is not the master of Assam, but originally, an outsider from Konouj. The Bodos or the Kacharis, the Koches, the Morans, the Chutias, the Ahoms, the Tribals and the Mongolians had kings

and kingdom in Assam, but there is no record in the history of an Assamese nationality and Assamese kingdom (Brahma, 1987).

Whether such statements are tenable or not is a different matter but the fact remains that among different ethnic groups in Assam, there is a passionate urge for self-determination. There has been a revolt against age-old bondage, impatience with stagnation and a thirst for rapid development based on a sense of identity. Surprisingly, though it may seem, while the dominant Assamese middle class have been suffering from a sense of neglect, discrimination and apathy of the central government, they at the same time fail to realise that the indigenous ethnic groups have also been suffering from a similar sense of 'neglect and discrimination' of the Assamese ruling class. As a result, the ethnic groups in Assam have been launching movements demanding either for the creation of separate or autonomous State on the basis of their lingo-cultural identities or for special constitutional safeguards of their respective identities.

IV

At this stage, it is worthwhile to mention that there are certain historical reasons for the hegemonic position of the Assamese ruling class. There has been hardly any significant growth of a regional bourgeois in the region. The late emergence of educated elite among other ethnic groups facilitated the upper caste dominant Assamese middle class to acquire the hegemonic position in Assam. The nationalism, which developed in Assam, grew under the leadership of this class, and therefore, it became the dominant nationality in this region. As a result, the ideas, values and culture of this class came to be imposed on other ethnic communities.

However, the cultural and ethnic issues are inextricably linked with the economic issues. It is not within the purview of the Assamese ruling class to make the ethnic group to be equal partners of the dominant section of the society. What they can do is to give certain concession to backward classes and share political power with them. In that case, a section of the class may enjoy certain privileges no doubt, but the basic problem will continue to exist as the opportunities are bound to be limited. Whatever privileges would be available; these will be enjoyed by a section of the emerging elite of the respective communities. These will never reach to its entire mass. Thus, there will be increasing unemployment and frustration even among the rank and file of the nascent middle class of the ethnic communities. The consciousness alone will not solve their basic problems, as they will still be within the same bureaucratic capitalist system which results in uneven economic development at various levels. It is therefore, necessary to think of a permanent solution to the problems, which requires a drastic change of the basic socio-economic structure of the country.

References

Brahma, U. 1987. '*An appeal to join All Bodo Students Union mass revolution*', A leaflet issued by Upendranath Brahma, President, ABSU on 9 August, 1987.

Deori, B. 1941. '*Debates of the Assam Legislative Council*', Volume V, No. 1, pp. 372-374, 18 June 1941.

Dutta, P.S. 1990. *Ethnic Movement in Poly-cultural Assam*, p. 16, New Delhi: Vikas Publishing House.

Gohain, H. 1991a. 'Assam and crisis of democracy', *The Telegraph,* 7th February, 1991.

Gohain, H. 1991b. 'Assamese nationality and tribal anxieties', *The Telegraph,* Calcutta Edition, 8th February, 1991.

Kachari Jubak Sanmilani. 1928. *Memorandum of the Kachari Community before the Simon Commission,* 14th September 1928.

Phukon, G. 2003. *Ethnicisation of Politics in North East India,* New Delhi.

6 Ethnicity and Identity Formation of the Mishings of Assam

Lohit Hazarika

"The intellectual history of the term 'ethnicity' is relatively short. Prior to the 1970s, there was little mention of it in anthropological literature and textbooks contained no definition of the term" as Despres (1975); and Cohen (1978) are quoted in the writing of Sokolovskii and Tishkov (2003: 190). They observed, "Since the mid-1970s, the concept has acquired strategic significance within anthropological theory partly as a response to the changing post-colonial geopolitics and the rise of ethnic minorities' activism in many industrial States. The shift has resulted in a proliferation of theories of ethnicity, explaining such diverse phenomena as social and political change, identity formation, social conflict, race relation, nation building, assimilation etc."

An ethnic group may be defined as group of individuals with a shared sense of peoplehood based on presumed shared socio-cultural experiences and similar physical characteristics. Such groups may be viewed by their members and outsiders as religious, racial, National, linguistic and geographical ones (Deshefsky, 1976).

Identity formation may be viewed from the global tendency to assert proto-nationalism or sub-nationalism. Baisya (1977) observes "Ethnocentrisms among some 300 tribal groups still using 50 different languages has found resurgent awareness and assertion there in the USA since the sixties of the present century. Tribal movement in India now coined a new perspective that movement for identity formation, started towards the second half of the nineteenth century. As early as 1947, the Jharkhand and Chhattishgarh tribes started agitation for separate States which ultimately gave dividends towards the end of the twentieth century. The north eastern states or undivided Assam was also not lagging behind. The all Assam Ahom Association was formed in 1910. In that time, some other ethnic groups like the Kacharis, Koch Rajbonshis, Chutiya and Motok constituted Sammelans and later on, they began to raise their demands under the banner of All Assam Plains Tribal League in 1937. During thirties of the twentieth century, a few other ethnic groups tried to assert their separate identities. They were Khasi National Conference, Garo National Conference, Mizo Union and Naga National Council (Bhuyan, 1980).

"What precisely is at issue when we use terms such as ethnicity or identity? Then 'consciousness of the kind' has long been an attribute of human groups, be these tribal; or national communities. This 'consciousness' arising out of sharing a common habitat and culture-including language and social traditions-gives the tribe or the nation the resources developing a common identity so essential for unified action as a group (Singh and Bhagabati,1982:496).

Articulation of ethnic identity can be perceived as a historical process, which combines both intentional and unintentional ways of behavioural patterns. Ethnic identity can also be changed as a sequel to historical social transformation. Further, he added that the consolidation of self-consciously articulated cultural practices and greater inclination towards cultural past are the obvious markers of ethnic boundary (Chaudhuri, 2002).

"Ethnic consciousness is not clearly something that is inborn but rather a constituent of many levels of identification and feelings" (Owen, 1975).

II

The Mishings (referred as Miris in the Scheduled Tribe list of Assam) constitute the second largest group of Schedule Tribe (Plains) of Assam. They are mainly concentrated in the riverside areas of Lakhimpur, Dibrugarh, Dhemaji, Sibsagar, Jorhat and Sonitpur districts of Assam. Stray pockets of the tribe are located in Golaghat district also. In spite of changes all round, the community has been able to preserve most of the traditional culture intact. They claim they had self-governing system during British rule and prior to that during Ahom rule; they enjoyed a great deal of autonomy (Kuli, 1998). The Mishing inhabited areas of

Murkongselek, Jonai and Sadiya maintained self-rule till 1911 although Assam was brought under the British rule in 1826 as per the treaty of Yandaboo (Pegu, 1998). "It is truism that the Mishing were originally a hill tribe within the ranges of the Abor, Miri and Mishmi hill of the erstwhile NEFA (North East Frontier Agency) now known as Arunachal Pradesh. The exact date of their migration to the plains is still shrouded. It is believed that they came down to the plains on the eve of the dissolution of the Chutiya dynasty" (Bordoloi and Sarma Thakur, 1987). As per 2001 census, their population was 5,87,310 (Male – 2,99,790 and Female – 2,87,520) consisting of 17.76 per cent of the total tribal population of the State. They belong to the Tibeto Burman linguistic family having Mongoloid morphological features. The Mishings are simple and straightforward and visitors are pleased at their hospitality. Gait (1963) observes, "The Miris are found both in the plains where they are peaceable British subjects and also in the hills to the north where they are quiet and inoffensive."

The Indian Confederation of Indigenous and Tribal People (ICITP), North East Zone observed that it is the right time to make a strong determination to find out amicable and lasting peace in the region. ICITP believes that the peace cannot be enforced by force. Self-determination should be based on people's right to their own land, freedom of speech and enjoyment of all other fundamental rights. It also added that communities must have power to negotiate peace through political, cultural and social discourse. It has been referred on UNESCO safeguarding of the intangible Cultural Heritage that was signed at 32nd session of UNESCO in Paris on 17th October, 2003. It includes the domain of knowledge and practices concerning nature and universe. The changing development paradigms that considered intellectual and spiritual tradition of the indigenous and local people's is base for the rights to self-determination.

In the following pages, we are trying to discuss the causes of ethnic identity formation of the Mishing tribe.

Since hoary past, Assam has been ungrudgingly providing shelter to numerous ethnic groups having their diverse socio-cultural life. The unique capacity of this eastern part of India to absorb heterogeneous groups coming through centuries and forming a cohesive society has been largely appreciated in various forums. However, over the decades, particularly in the post-Independence period, the fission process appeared causing a breach in the age-old amity and good neighbourliness. The ethno-political conflict and autonomy and the Sixth Schedule demands from various ethnic groups raised new dimensions of ethnic identifications and revivalism among the groups. The phenomena has been studied by the anthropologists and historians over the decades but none has been able to explain whether the movements are 'Spontaneous' or created by the vested interests of the elites of the concerned groups.

III

Methods of Study

The present chapter is based on both primary and secondary sources of data. The primary data were collected through Structured Interview Schedule in Lakhimpur, Dhamaji and Jorhat Districts of Assam. There were three schedules. All together, 25 leaders and 150 of persons from 30 selected villages were interviewed. In-depth case studies were collected to understand processes of consolidation. The secondary data were collected from various records and documents preserved in University libraries, magazines, books, leaflets and memorandums submitted by the Mishing leaders from time to time projecting their demands. The fieldwork was done in 2008- 2009.

IV

Discussion

Former General Secretary of Takam Mishing Porin Kebang and President Mishing Mibak Kebang, Dr Ranoj Pegu (1998) mentions that the Mishing had their self- governing pattern of an administration till the annexation of Assam by the British colonial rules in 1826. Even the great Ahom rulers who ruled Assam till the annexation by the British for 600 years, did not interfere the self-rule although they had no king or chief. Even after annexation of Assam, the major portion of the territory, especially, far flung Murrkang Selek; Jonai and Sadia areas were enjoying self-rule till 1911. The colonial rulers did not think to improve the socio-economic conditions of the Mishing; rather the areas were amalgamated with heterogeneous population. Some of the villages were tagged to Balipara Frontier Tract, Sadiya Frontier Tract and

Lakhimpur Frontier Tract. Besides, few more villages were kept under British provincial administration. The 1935 Act created the NEFA under the Excluded area category and good number of the Mishings was tagged to this Agency.

Ranoj Pegu (ibid) further referred that after independence, Government of India has reviewed the entire tribal policy of the British Government. A committee was formed under the chairmanship of Gopinath Bordoloi and the report of the Committee was submitted to the Advisory Committees on fundamental rights, minorities, and tribal and excluded areas of the Constituent Assembly. As per recommendation of the Bordoloi Committee, eight autonomous district councils were constituted under the Sixth Schedule. These are: United Khasi and Jayantia Hills, the Garo Hills, the Lushai Hills, the Naga Hills, the North Chachar Hills, the Mikir Hills, North East Frontier Tract including Balipara Frontier Tract, Abor Hills and Mishimi Hills, and the Naga Tribal Areas. The Mishing of the plains were left out of the above arrangement and development of the areas became the responsibility of the Government of Assam. The Report of the sub-committee, *inter alia*, contained as follows:

> "The population of the plains tribes, which is being gradually assimilated into the population of the plains, should for all purposes be treated as minority. Measures for protection of their lands are also in our view for necessary action..... We have also provided that administration of the areas is to be brought under the Provincial Administration in future and should also be similar to that of the existing hill districts."

Incidentally, it may be mentioned that the last line of the above report contains the autonomy status including the Sixth Schedule based on which the tribes are demanding Sixth Schedule status.

Identity and Ethnicity Formation: The Contemporary Impetus

M.C. Paul (1992) pointed out that severe socio-economic deprivation and deep feelings of discontentment since long among the plain tribes have acted as a catalyst to throw them in to the vortex of the movements. In other words, the ethnic movement among the plains tribes of Assam is a product of the inner contradictions in the socio-economic and political system. They are increasingly aware of the oppressions and injustice and becoming restless. The articulated educated and conscious sections of the plain tribals are now leading the tribes to fry out their plight.

Judging from socio-anthropological angle, the tribal identity formation takes place mainly due to economic deprivation (Danda, 1991). Deprivation or dissatisfactions very often lead to identity formation. Inequality in the society breeds dissatisfaction and the outburst of such age long deprivity finds expression in identity formation. Poor and slow economic developments, vested interests, exploitation of leaders— even from among the elite tribal leaders— are determining factors for developing a sense of identity formation among the ethnic groups. The paternalistic attitude of the colonist rulers and even of planners and administrators of post- independence period contributed largely in the formation of the contemporary tribal identity.

In my study areas, the villagers are facing many problems in their locality. Flood (23 villages, i.e., 76.00 per cent) is a major problem, followed by erosion (16 villages i.e., 53.33 per cent), lack of roads (21 villages), electricity (20 villages), health facilities, drinking water (22 villages i.e., 73.33 per cent), fair price shop, unemployment, etc. They found themselves unable to stand up against their counterparts in other societies and thus lead to movements on their ethnic identity.

In contemporary times, it was observed that the positive interaction with other ethnic groups encouraged an ethnic group to assert identity. The Bodo movement became a torchbearer for Mishings. After long and tenuous agitation programmes; submission of Memorandums, official dialogues with dignitaries of central Government, a Memorandum of Settlement known as Bodo Accord was passed where by a Bodoland Autonomous Council (BAC) was constituted within the State of Assam. In this context, we may refer to the movement launched by the Plain Tribal Council of Assam for Union territory status or Bodoland Territorial Council status. In all the memorandums of P.T.C.A., reference is invariably made about the plain tribes, in general, and the Mishing have had moral and practical support of the P.T.C.A. programmes. Thus, the idea of movement for self-determination had its roots in the P.T.C.A. demands.

Lower Social Status

It is observed that although the Mishing declared themselves to be Hindus, yet, they are not in a position to attain position of honour in the society at large. Some of them declare themselves to be Vaisnavites, yet they have faith in the traditional religious beliefs and practices. Very often, they are required to satisfy inquisitive persons about their dualism in respect of religious beliefs vis-a-vis Vaisnavism. Instead of appreciating the endeavour of the Mishings, some persons irritate them affecting the bond of togetherness. Deogaonkar (1992) is of the opinion that the history of tribal movement shows that, tribals, often have been exploited by the so-called "mainstream" which holds power over them, for their selfish ends. These power holders consider the resistance by the tribal for self-protection as an affront. This stimulates a political process, which leads for fighting for their interests, which leads to the movement for autonomy.

In an interview, Mr. J. Pegu (Assistant General Sectary, Mishing Bane Kebang), quoting from the interview of a Satradhikar of Majuli of a local television channel (News Live) said, "The Satradhikar had admitted that the Mishings are neglected and the people of Assam did not understand the sentiment of the former". Pegu added, "...in 1924, in the Cotton College, the tribal students were allotted a particular hostel, and the higher caste students in other hostel. The students of higher caste used to sprinkle sacred water to clean self when the tribal students visited them in the hostel." He was remembering discriminating behavior of the Majuli Satradhikar, who used to keep the Mishings waiting outside unlike the higher caste. He felt that these age old reasons articulated voices of the tribes for ethnic identity formation.

Immigration

Former General Secretary of Takam Mishing Porin Kebang and President Mishing Mibak Kebang, Dr R. Pegu, pointed out that immigration is a strong cause, which forced them for identity formation movement. He discussed the following information to support his points.

The tribal people became restive when hordes of land hungry Mymensingias came in large numbers to Assam in search of land and by 1931, their number exceeded eight lakhs in the plains districts. Seeing the gravity of the situation, the then British Government had introduced the Line System demarcating areas beyond which immigrants were debarred from entry. But the system did not work as land settlement with immigrants increased from 481 thousand acres in 1930-31 to 5967 acres in 1940; in over a period of 20 years settlement of land with immigrants rose to 14,669 thousand acres in the Assam Valley (Census of India, 1951).

Immigration from Eastern Bengal started as early as 1911. The then superintendent of Census, Mr. Loyd comments like this "In 1911, few cultivators from Eastern Bengal had gone Goalpara. In the last decade 1911-21, the movement had extended far up the valley in the colonies now form an appreciable elements in population of all the four lower and central districts. Almost every train and steamer brings parties of these settlers and it seems likely that their march will extend further up the Brahmaputra Valley and away from river before lorry" (Census of India, A Report on Assam, 1921).

In 1931, the then Superintendent of Census, C.S. Mullan observed, "It is sad but by no means improbable that in another thirty years Sibsagar district will be the only part of Assam in which an Assamese will find himself at home" (Census Report of Assam, 1931). The same census report pointed out that the local indigenous people will face the crisis of identity if the flow is not restrained.

In 1937, the Government constituted a 'Line System' committee to review the working of the system. F.W. Hokenhull was the chairman. The committee recommended that instead of a line dividing the area of a village; a large unit of restriction should be adopted, such as, a *Mouzas* or a block of *Mouzas*, which were to be protected from encroachers. It may be noted that as a result of large scale encroachment of the Mymensingias, the tribal villagers were the worst victims. The tribal people feel that land is gift of nature like air or water and they, therefore, were not alert about the evil desire of the encroachers. Goswami (1986) opines, "To them, land for use can be obtained by fairly simple means of enjoying membership of a tribal group, membership of a kin group, residence in a village etc., but less frequently, through contractual relationships such as purchase pledge, loan, lease client ship or service."

The idea of forming Tribal Belts and Blocks was first conceived by the Congress coalition Ministry in 1939 when Gopinath Bordoloi took charge as "Prime Minister" (later changed to Chief Minister). A new chapter (Chapter X) was added to the Assam Land and Revenue Regulation 1886, known as Assam Act XV of 1947. Originally, 38 Belts and Blocks were created. "Today, there are 46 tribal Belts and Blocks" (Goswami, ibid).

"The partition of India gave a new dimension to the already overburdened population of Assam created by the influx of immigrant population from East Bengal. Refugees from East Pakistan entered Assam as Assam had to provide shelter to them on humanitarian grounds. According to a Census in 1949, 1,14,000 persons came to Assam with 24,600 families. There was strong anti-India and anti-Hindu atmosphere in East Pakistan and as a result of the infamous February-March happenings of 1950, another 2,74,455 refugees came to Assam. In order to provide accommodation, including their economic support, many areas of fallow lands, wasteland, grazing reserves and forestlands of tribal belts and blocks were opened for them."

Therefore, to protect their land and forest from the outsiders, the Mishing is inclined to their ethnic identity for Sixth Schedule status under the Constitution of India.

Assamese Language Act, 1960

The Mishings have their own language and distinctive culture. They voluntarily accepted Assamese language not only for expressing ideas to the non-Mishings but also for educating their children through Assamese medium. However, on October 10, 1960, the then Chief Minister of Assam brought the Assam Official Language Bill in the Assembly causing much tension to the ethnic groups of the State. The Assam Official Language Act of 1960 brought a rift with the Mishing society as they did not like forceful imposition of Assamese language. In 1972, Government of Assam directed the Gauhati and Dibrugarh University to introduce Assamese as medium of instruction in place of English. Again, the A.G.P. Government, just after assuming power, imposed Assamese language as compulsory third language on the non-Assamese medium secondary schools. The Secondary Board of Assam (SEBA) circulated the same on 28th February, 1986. There was widespread resentment against Assam government's language policy which went against the aspirations and ambitions of the tribal people. The Mishings, in fact, started a movement to revive their language, as the use of the language was limited due to 'Sanskritisation' or 'Hinduisation' process. Nath (1998) opines that, "the present Mishing language being a tribal language is a '*Mleecha Bhasa'* of Kubasha for the non-tribal Aryan speakers. The growing tribal consciousness towards the protection of their culture on the way to asserting their identity in the society has brought about a new dimension in the field of their cultivating own language. The ethnic organisations of the Mishing, like Mishing Agom Kebang (Mishing Sahitya Sabha) formed in April 1972, the Takam Mishing Porin Kebang (All Mishing Student Union) and the Bane Kebang (Mishing People's Conference) spearheaded the movement. As a result of the movement, Mishing language has been accepted as medium of instruction in class III and class IV of primary school since 1987.

The early Mishing mentors used 'Assamese script' and different organisations advised the Mishing to continue with the Assamese script. However, Mishing Agom Kebang and Takam Mishing Porin Kebang preferred Roman script. They also did not accept Pattanayak's (chairman of the one man committee determining script for Mishing) report where Assamese or Devnagari script was recommended. Roman script prevailed among the Mishings.

Educational Elite

Datta, 1993 observes, with emergence of a middle class through expansion of modern education and entry to jobs under colonial Administration, seeds of identity consciousness were sown. In addition, this very class of people played a pioneering role in unfolding, consolidating and then spreading an identity consciousness among the members of their own societies. Social discriminations, alleged superiority complex of the caste Hindu Assamese, and the caste-based social equations, gradually started pushing them away from whatever proximity might have been achieved with the core Assamese society. Gradually, the unsolved economic apprehension started getting a political direction. The atmosphere of neglect and indifference expedited the withdrawal process further. The hurt sentiments of the 'middle classes' realised that, without political power, no malady could be remedied and as a result bargaining for political power began."

In the post-independence period, due to large-scale interaction and expansion of educational facilities to the tribal people, Mishing community possesses quite a good number of educated persons and they no longer tolerate the injustices, maladministration and oppression. Identity formation has offered new dimensions to the exclusiveness of the ethnic group. To attain the goal, the educated section adopted different strategies. They formed different organisations to mobilise different sections of people. It is remarkable that the main objective of the Mishing elite section is to maintain distinct Mishing self-identity. The Mishing's first organisation was named as "Sadou Assam Miri Sanmilan" established in 1924 with the aim of bringing development to the problem-ridden society. However, after that the organisation was renamed as "Mishing Bane Kebang". Kebang is the traditional political organisation who looked upon all socio-political affairs of the Mishing society. They took the nomenclature to articulate all Mishing people to the organisation. This lead to the new ethnic identity formation of Mishing. TMPK also was first established in the name as 'Assam Miri Chatra Sonmilon'. In 1971, it was renamed as the 'Assam NEFA Mishing Chatra Sanmilon". In 1978, it was further renamed as "Sodou Assam Mishing Chatra Santha". Again, in the year 1985, it was assigned the name "Takam Mishing Porin Kebang" in Mishing language. "Mishing Agom Kebang" (MAK, Mishing Literary Society) was also established in the year 1972 to develop their language and literature. This organisation is giving a literary platform to educated section of people to discuss the problems and prospects of the Mishing people. The main aim of organisation is to develop their language and literature, which is obvious marker of an ethnic identity. Mishing Dirbi Kebang (MDK, Mishing Cultural Organisation) is an organisation formed for the cultural development of Mishing society in 1980. This organisation created an atmosphere where the cultural people of the community got an opportunity to sit together and bring out the rich culture from village to outside world. This makes the people feel proud of their culture and a sense of belongingness emerged, which is marker of an identity formation process. The Mishing Mimag Kebang (MMK, Mishing Action Committee) was formed completely with a political aim and agenda in 1986. MMK's main aim is to get full political autonomy for Mishing by adopting various political means. At last, they formed Takam Mishing Mimo Kebang (TMMK, Mishing Woman Organisation) to associate the woman section with various development activities of Mishing. The main aim of this organisation is to fight for the woman of Mishing, in particular and work with the Mishing, in general.

All the organisations take various programmes and agenda based on their constitution and by-laws for the identity formation process.

Constitutional Provision

To meet the aspirations of the tribal people, to safeguard their economic interests and their traditional customary way of life, and to pursue them to accede to the Indian Union, the constituent Assembly set up an advisory committee known as the North-East Frontier (Assam) tribal areas sub-committee with Gopinath Bordoloi as its chairman. The concept of Autonomous Tribal Council was evolved and the committee formulated the Sixth Schedule of the Constitution. The Sixth Schedule to the Constitution of India gave legal sanction to identity movements by providing a political mechanism in the hands of rising middle class in hills. The Sixth Schedule was chosen as a means of quieting the political opposition of the emerging middle class in the hills by proliferation of offices of profit. The Khasis, the Garos, the Pnars and the Mizos took advantage in the form of District Council. This influences the Mishing to fight for the Sixth Schedule status.

Distinction from Assamese Culture

Phukan (1993), in his book, is of the opinion that most of the tribes of the plains are culturally less distinct from the Assamese caste Hindus than the hill tribes because of the relatively greater interaction between them through the centuries. The tribal communities though contributed for the growth and development of the Assamese culture, yet a section of the tribal elite felt that, as they are different from the Assamese caste Hindus, they have to preserve their distinct tribal identity. In an interview, Mr S. Tayeng, Vice-President, Takam Mishing Porin Kebang, Central Body expresed "We want autonomy for the survival as distinct ethnic group." Bhagabati (1982) viewed that, "many of the tribes now find the Assam Hindu model rather inadequate. Instead, tribal identity is asserted and cultivated through revival re-interpretation of tribal festivals and other aspects of culture. On the cultural front, languages have emerged as one of the major issues among those tribes who are so long sub-served in the wider Assam Nationality". The early Mishing mentors used 'Assamese Script' and different organisations advised the Mishing to continue with the Assamese script. However, Mishing Agom Kebang and Takam Mishing Porin Kebang preferred Roman script as opposed to Assamese or Devnagari script. Roman script prevailed among the Mishings". Mr J. Pegu, Assistant General Secretary, Mishing Bene Kebang, in an interview said, "The Mishing is a rich language; to protect and preserve it, they formed Mishing Agom Kebang."

They feel that new introductions to their age long traditional culture brings more harm than good to the socio-economic set up. The traditional values, modes and morals, material culture, belief system, etc., of the tribals are subjected to pressure of change. As a result, when damage is already done to the socio-cultural fabric, the tribal groups seek to reaffirm their social identity which Rothschild (1981) refers, "modernisation mobilises ethnic groups and converts them into active politico-cultural collectivities".

It was assumed that, due to ethnic identity formation of the Mishing, the age-old tie with Assamese would effect adversely. However, 138 (92.00 per cent) informants of my study felt that there is no such fear of losing good relations with the Assamese. Only five informants opine that it will distance the Mishings from the Assamese while seven informants have preferred not to comment. The TMPK leaders, in answering a question, opine that a strong and developed Mishing tribe will contribute in a better way to the grater Assamese nationality.

References

Baisya, P. 1977. 'From tribal belt to autonomous council: Genesis of the leap in autonomous district council', In L.S. Gassah (Ed): *Autonomous District Council,* New Delhi: Omsons Publications.

Bhagabati, A.C.1992. 'Tribal transformation in Assam and North East India: An appraisal of emerging ideological dimension', In B. Chaudhuri (Ed): *Tribal Transformation in India,* pp. 487-509, Vol. III, New Delhi: Inter India Publications.

Bhattarchajee, C. 1996. *Ethnicity and Autonomy Movement (Case of Boro-Kacharis of Assam),* New Delhi: Vikas Publishing House Pvt. Ltd.

Bhuyan A.C. 1980. *Political History of Assam.* pp. 311-312, Part III, Guwahati: Government of Assam.

Bordoloi, B.N., G.C. Sarmah Thakur and M.C. Saikia. 1987. *Tribes of Assam* (Part-I), Guwahati : Assam Tribal Research Institute.

Census of India 1921, Government of India.

Census of India 1931, Government of India.

Census of India 1951, Government of India.

Census of India 1991, Government of India.

Census of India 2001, Government of India.

Chaudhuri, S.K. 2000. 'Articulation and maintenance in the Maan ethnic identity', *Journal of Anthropological Survey of India,* 50: 73-84.

Danda, A.K. 1991. *Ethnicity in India.* New Delhi: Inter-India Publications.

Datta, P.S. 1993. *Autonomy Movement in Assam (Documents),* New Delhi: Omsons Publishing House.

Deogaonkar, S.G. 1992. 'Tribal movements'. In B. Choudhury (Ed): *The Tribal Transformation in India: Ethno Politics and Identity Crisis.* Vol. III. New Delhi: Inter India Publication.

Deshefsky, A. 1976. *Ethnic Identity in Society,* Chicago College Publishing Company.

Gait, E.A. 1963. *A History of Assam* (Reprint) 3rd edition, Calcutta.

Glazer Nathan and D.P. Moynihan. 1975. *Ethnicity,* U.S.A.: Harvard University Press.

Kuli, J. J. 1998. *The Mishings—Their History and Culture,* Guwahati: Ayir Publications.

LI:SANG. 2006. Mouthpiece of Takam Mishing Poring Kebang, Amarpur, Sadiya.

LI:SANG, 2009, Mouthpiece of Takam Mishing Poring Kebang , Dhemaji, Assam.

Mahapatra, L.K. 1992. 'Social movement among the tribes in Eastern India'. In Buddhadev Choudhury (Ed): *The Tribal Transformation in India: Ethno Politics and Identity Crisis,* Vol. III, New Delhi: Inter India Publications.

Nath, D. 1998. 'The Mishings in the history of Assam. In J. J. Kuli (Ed): *The Mishings - Their History and Culture.* Guwahati: Ayir Publications.

Owen, N.H. 1975. 'Land, politics and ethnicity in a Carib Indian community', *Ethnology,* 14, 4: 385-393.

Paul, M.C. 1992. 'Udhayachal movement, plains tribals and social structure in Assam valley: A sociological exploration'. In B. Choudhury (Ed): *The Tribal Transformation in India: Ethno Politics and Identity Crisis*, Vol. III. New Delhi: Inter India Publications.

Pegu, R. 1993. 'Autonomy movement of the Mishing people'. In J.J. Kuli (Ed): *The Mishings - Their History and Culture,* Guahati: Ayir Publication.

Phukan, G. 1984. *Assam's Attitude to Federalism.* New Delhi: Sterling Publishers.

Rothschild, Joseph. 1981. *Ethno Politics-Conceptual Framework.* New York.

Sen Chaudhuri, S. 2004. *The Bodo Movement and Women Participation.* New Delhi: Mittal Publications.

Sengupta, Sarthak. 1994. *Tribal Situation in North-East India,* New Delhi: Inter-India Publications.

Sokolovskii, S. and V. Tiskov. 2003. 'Ethnicity'. In A. Barnard and J. Spencer (Ed): *Encyclopedia of Social and Cultural Anthropology,* London: Routledge.

7 Aspiration for an Ethnic Identity—Evolved or Created?

A Question Asked in the Context of Assam

Pranami Garg

North East India, and specifically Assam, is the homeland of different ethnic groups with a variety of cultures and speaking different languages and dialects. Many scholars consider it as the melting pot of diverse races, castes, religions, languages and cultures. Inter-ethnic conflicts and struggle for identity among the ethnic groups too are not new but a frequently occurring phenomenon. However, such conflicts have become more common and all pervading at present. It is largely, due to over politicisation of the factors composing the ethnic identities. Politicisation takes place at two levels-on one level, politicisation of people's cultural, linguistic and most importantly, ethnic sentiments resulting in ethnic conflicts, and at another level, politicisation by the decision makers as part of their efforts to find a solution to the conflict. This chapter tries to focus on these two aspects of politicisation that are playing a pivotal role in making the identity crises and conflicts an enduring phenomenon in Assam.

Ethnicity and Aspiration for Identity

Ethnicity stands for a group's way of conceptualising and relating to society. It welds together individuals who share a history, culture and community, who have an amalgam of language, religion and regional belonging in common and perhaps most critical of all; they feel that they come from the same stock (Wilson and Frederiksen, 1991: 2). Though the term ethnicity is of recent origin, its idea has been present since long. Its probable first use by David Reisman in 1953 only renamed an already existing and recognised phenomenon. People have identified themselves with particular cultures through processes like acculturation, integration and assimilation. Ethnic identity on the other hand is an affiliative construct, where individuals view themselves and others view them as belonging to a particular cultural group (Trimble and Dickson, 2005). The growth of the spirit of ethnicity or ethnic self-assertion among various groups leads to the aspiration for a distinct identity for themselves.

Ethnic identity has both objective and subjective connotations. Objectively, it is "primordial affinities and attachments", and "subjectively, it is an activated primordial consciousness" (Subba, 1996: 39). While Issacs (1975) and Greeley (1974) supported the objective concept, Geertz (1975) emphasised the latter and Van den Berghe argues in favour of combining the two (Subba, 1996: 39). The ethnic groups with a small population and low exposure to development tend to suffer from an identity crisis. The aspirations for an independent ethnic identity lead to the formation of a nation within a nation through various ways including ethnic struggles and violence.

Identity Crisis among the Ethnic Communities in Assam

Assam—one of the eight States of North East India— is enclosed by Bangladesh, Bhutan and Tibet and linked with mainland India by a narrow corridor between Bangladesh, Bhutan and Nepal. The population of Assam consists of the inhabitants who migrated into the region at various periods of history from Tibet, Burma, Thailand, Bengal and elsewhere. Over time, they got integrated as a population and have given birth to the greater Assamese nation. Present day Assam roughly covers the area ruled by the 'native' ethnic groups, the Ahoms, Bodos, Koch, Mataks and Chutiya and different branches of Kacharis such as Dimasa, Sonowal and Thengal.

Opinions on the Assamese nation today range from those who subscribe to the view that there is no Assamese identity, to those who claim that such an identity, to those who think that it is in process of formation or those who say that it is not restricted only to the native speakers of the Assamese language but embrace all those who come within the broader fold of Assamese culture and those who think that it belongs only to the ethnic Assamese (Misra, 2001). The aspiration of a separate Assamese identity has its origin in the colonial discriminatory treatment of the region. From 1874, the North East formed part of the Bengal Presidency. A feeling grew in Assam that it was treated as an adjunct and a subordinate area of Bengal. Such discrimination continued also after independence. The discriminatory attitude of the Centre becomes clear from a letter written by Sardar Patel to Pandit Nehru in 1950: "Our Northern or North-eastern approaches consist of Nepal, Bhutan, Sikkim, Darjeeling and the tribal areas of Assam. From the point of view of communication, they are weak spots........The contact of these areas with us, is by no means close and intimate. The people inhabiting these portions have no established loyalty or devotion to India." (Subba, 1991: 97).

However, the social minorities within Assam felt discriminated against. They struggled against the British colonialist as well as the Indian dominant groups among whom were the ethnic Assamese. With the Bengal Eastern Frontier Regulation of 1873, a Line System was introduced on the pretext of protecting the minority indigenous ethnic groups in the hill areas of Assam by restricting outsiders' entry, business activities, land transactions and settlement. For the same purpose, in 1935, the hill areas were demarcated and divided into "excluded areas" and "partially excluded areas" (Chaube, 1999). The former fell under direct British jurisdiction and the latter were given a limited representative system under British administrative control.

The dominant classes in mainland India as well as in Assam thought that this colonial history of separation and isolation from the rest of India created a problem for the national formation and integration of independent India. In the region, a sense of incompatibility grew into one of resentment against being made a part of India, and an anti-India sentiment emerged among some communities. Thus, the process of alienation did not stop after independence. Some, like the Nagas, declared their independence because they felt that Mainland India did not understand their identity (Sanyu, 1996: 115-116). These feelings had to be dealt with.

To deal with this feeling of discrimination, the Constitution of India contained a special provision in the form of the Sixth Schedule for the administration of the "tribal" areas. It was meant to protect their communities in the Hill areas of the North East. Under it, the "tribal" areas in the North East were divided into two parts, Part A and Part B. Part A has Autonomous Districts administered by the Government of Assam, with a limited representation in the State

Legislative Assembly and in the National Parliament. The Governor of Assam acting as Agent of the President of India administered Part B. The United Khasi and Jaintia Hills District, the Garo Hills District, the Lushai Hills District, the Naga Hills District, the North Cachar Hills District, and the Mikir Hills District were placed in Part A and the North East Frontier Tract, the Balipara Frontier Tract, the Tirap Frontier Tract, the Abor Hill and Mishmi Hills Districts and the Naga Tribal Area came under Part B. Tripura and Manipur were made special administrative regions under the control of the Central Government. The reorganisation of the States on linguistic terms further aggravated the scene. The tribal areas under the Sixth Schedule got statehood one by one. Thus, Assam was broken up and North East India became seven States.

The process of being divided on the line of ethnicity did not stop here. The aspiration for a distinct identity among the ethnic groups resulted in a number of movements demanding autonomy. As a result, at present there are eight Autonomous Councils in the State. Today, in Assam, there are either movements for separate States or autonomy on the part of different ethnic groups. These groups had come together during the Assam Movement 1979-85, but the Assam Accord 1985, mentioned only the ethnic Assamese. That alienated the groups that had identified themselves with a common Assamese identity (Roy, 1995: 41-43). Slowly the non-Assamese groups developed a desire to be separate and hence have come up with a struggle for a separate identity. Why did that happen? Its answer rests in the two-way politicisation of the ethnicity elements and State role along with the element of deprivation and domination.

Why Ethnicity?

An identity is born because of a variety of factors. Every ethnic group has its own distinct culture, language or dialect and traditional institutions. The fact of belonging to one group often gives rise to fellow feelings and sentiments. Factors like the desire to preserve one's culture and traditional institutions, preventing them from being assimilated with the dominant culture, fear of being deprived of what is one's due and exploitation of resources by outsiders make such sentiments stronger. For Baruah (2004: 19), "identity is directly related to the emergence of educated elite in the concerned community." In the absence of any other major social force, such an elite comes to acquire a hegemonic position in the community, perpetuates its hegemony and mobilises the community on communal lines. Das (2004: 70) finds factors such as a desire for self-expression, perceived discrimination and injustice; aspirations of minor politicians, better economic development of neighbouring small States are responsible for the rise of sub-national and ethnic movements in Assam.

The stronger groups being unable or unwilling or both often do not take cognizance of even the legitimate needs and aspirations of weaker ethnic groups (Datta, 1990:39). Such intolerance and imperviousness leads to the growth of a feeling of discrimination and alienation on the part of smaller group. The dominant group possesses a tendency to brand all group aspirations and demands as anti-national or secessionist without going into their merits or demerits. The smaller groups get lost in the process of forced assimilation in the name of accommodation and integration. This gives rise to the desire for self-expression and an identity separate from that of the dominant groups.

Ethnic Identity and Politicisation

Along with such factors of ethnic identity formation, a crisis is created by politicisation. The very crisis arising out of cultural, economic and linguistic deprivation grows and develops into a conflict through political interference. Politics is about the 'transformative capacity' of social agents, agencies and institutions, while politicisation implies inclusion of certain issues in its domain. As per Oxford Advanced Dictionary, politicisation implies the process of becoming politically conscious or organised. As the meaning of the term indicates, politicisation itself is not a negative concept. It helps the ethnic groups to grow conscious of their existence and rights. However, over-interference of politics in the phenomenon of an identity crisis makes the situation worse. The present situation of identity crisis, social formation and rise of sub-nationalism is largely due to political orientation in the wrong direction.

Politics plays a two-way role in ethnicity and rise of sub-nationalism. Firstly, politics of recognition and representation has encouraged the growth of the ethnic groups' demand for a distinct set-up which results in the formation of sub-nationalism or a nation within a nation. At this stage, it is important to recognise the distinctness of these groups. However, when it is perceived as a favour granted or a right acquired through a political struggle, the State policy of recognition of traditional institutions and representation of the ethnic groups in the decision-making bodies can nourish stronger sentiments and emotions of ethnicity among other groups. Its outcome can be noticed at various levels. At the institutional level, as Dev *et al.*, (n.d) opine, the ensuing politics of 'recognition' employed by the federal State have fashioned a multiplicity of institutions which contest with similar institutions of other groups and also with the structures of the State and autonomous institutions. In such circumstances, Benedict Anderson's (1991) phrase 'imagined community' seems to become a reality. Ethnic sentiments, emotions related to their culture, language, symbols etc. and politics of recognition and representation come together to give birth to an image of their communion or nationhood which can also be described as sub-nationalism. In fact, there is a need to "imagine" a multi-ethnic, multi-cultural and multi-linguistic integrated Assamese society, but politicisation has turned this imagination into a conflict and crisis.

Secondly, the presence of political interference is again felt when this sub-nationalism grows to its full capacity causing a threat to the State. As Dov Ronen (1986: 1) suggests, "ethnicity is politicised into the ethnic factor when an ethnic group is in conflict with the political elite over such issues as the use of limited resources or the allocation of benefits. Tambiah (1989: 339) reiterates the same when he says that, "central problems posed by our present phrase of ethnic conflicts are startlingly different arising out of an intensified 'politicisation of ethnicity' and ensuing in conflicts between member groups of a State and polity, which itself is thought to be in crisis ('the crisis of the State')." With this backdrop, it will not be unnatural or surprising to ask whether the aspiration for distinct ethnic identity is evolved over time or is created on behalf of the State, the politicians and the leaders of the ethnic groups. What are the benefits of such politicisation?

Aspirations for Separate Identity and Politicisation

The first instance of politicisation and alienation of ethnic groups from the greater Assamese identity can be traced to the politicisation of their identity aspiration. Bora (2006: 461) finds three reasons for the identity crisis of the ethnic groups in Assam. They are— emergence of consciousness of being different from the group under whose identity, it continued for so long, feeling of getting segregated and discriminated against and desire for bigger share in power wielding machinery — for more economic, educational and job facilities. The discriminatory policies of the Centre and political aspirations of the groups, which form an integral part of the game of politics, play the chief role in emergence of new ethnic identities.

Besides, the vested political or power interests of the ethnic groups are fulfilled through the sentiments of culture, language and symbols. As Bora (2006: 464) illustrates, the political ambitions and organisations of other interests become easy at the backdrop of cultural identity as cultural identity is an emotional and sentimental issue that evokes mass support. All the autonomy movements in Assam have started with the premise that immense discrimination has been done to them by the dominant group as well as the Centre and they should get autonomy; while they end with the grant of autonomy in a specific area, which fulfils their craving for power. The Koch Rajbangshi struggle is a current example.

Conflict Resolution and Politicisation

The role played by politics in the desire for identity does not end with the moulding of public sentiment in a definite direction or birth of the demand for separate identity or autonomy by each ethnic group. It continues throughout the process of conflict, which is an offshoot of the aspiration for identity. The conflict arises out of deprivation and self-assertion. It is politicised by the elements that are unable to find a solution to the till today. One of its main reasons is the policies and actions of the government. The State response to the Bodo, Sonowal-Kachari, Rabha-Hasong and other movements is bureaucratic. In fact, the British legacy of isolating and either dominating the conflicting groups with an iron hand without taking into account their support base or postponing the possibility of solution, and compromising after being unable to cater to the problem finds expression through the actions of the government. The Bodoland Accord and declaration of BTC is an example for such bureaucratic behaviour of the State.

Besides, it has also been observed that certain incentives allow the struggle to continue, while disincentives in resolving it, both on the part of the decision-makers and on the part of the movement leaders. While political leaders would no more be able to project the issue in their election manifestos, the leaders of the struggle would cease to act as a pressure group once the conflict is resolved. Neither party wants to thus lose its power. For example, the prime issues including economic exploitation, discrimination and crisis of identity among the Bodos have not been solved even after the signing of the Peace Accord. When one group seems to reach a solution, its competing groups raise them in order to keep the issue alive.

Conclusion

This chapter has attempted to deal with the ethnic identity issue in Assam. It has looked at the double identity issue of the ethnic Assamese versus the Centre and the minorities within the State vis-à-vis the ethnic Assamese. While discussing the conflicts that ensure from it, a doubt has been expressed as to whether an identity crisis on the part of different ethnic groups is evolved or created. Though it is not possible to answer it in a single sentence, one can summarise it by saying that the age-old suppression and exploitation of the ethnic groups, linguistically and culturally, by the dominant group generates the need of an identity. Its politicisation gives it a shape of a conflict. Giving the groups their due share in the development of the State, and recognition to their culture, traditions, language, etc., is an urgent need. Nation-building is not possible without recognising the specificities of each component. The solution is integration and not assimilation though some dominant groups demand it. Political interference can play a uniting role in resolving the conflicts and the crisis for identity. To deal with it, one has to find a solution to the basic demands of the ethnic groups.

References

Anderson, B. 1991. *Imagined Communities: Reflections on the Origin and Spread on Nationalism*, London: Verso.

Baruah, A. K. 2004. 'Identity crisis in North East India and its consequences'. In Thomas Vattathara and Elizabeth George (Eds): *Peace Initiatives—A North East India Perspective*, pp. 17-27, Guwahati: Don Bosco Publications.

Bora, S. 2006. 'Ethnic Struggles in Assam: An observation'. In Prasenjit Biswas and C. Joshua Thomas (Eds.): *Peace in India's North-East Meaning, Metaphor and Method, Essays of Concern and Commitment,* pp. 459-468, New Delhi: Regency Publications.

Chaube, S.K. 1999. *Hill Politics in Northeast India.* Hyderabad: Orient Longman.

Das, H.N. 2004. 'Ethnicity and insurgency in the north-eastern region of India', in Thomas Vattathara and Elizabeth George (Eds.) *: Peace Initiatives - A North East India Perspective,* pp. 66-83, Guwahati: Don Bosco Publications.

Datta, B. 1990. 'Ethnicity, nationalism and sub-nationalism, with special reference to North-East India'. In B. Pakem (Ed): *Nationality, Ethnicity and Cultural Identity in North-East India.* pp. 36-44. New Delhi: Omsons Publications.

Dev, R.; A.K Baruah and M. Sarmah. (n.d). 'Liberal democracy, traditional institutions and politics of representation - Analysing the Nongkynrih Shnong Dorbar', Shillong: NEIDS.

Misra, U. 2001. *The Transformation of Assamese Identity.* Shillong: North East India History Association.

Ronen, D.1986. 'Ethnicity, politics and development: An introduction'. In Dennis L. Thompson and D. Ronen (Eds.): *Ethnicity, Politics and Development,* pp. 1 – 9, Boulder: Lynne Rienner Publishers.

Roy, A. 1995. *The Boro Imbroglio.* Guwahati: Spectrum Publishers.

Sanyu, V. 1996. *A History of Nagas and Nagaland: Dynamics of Traditional Village Formation.* New Delhi: Commonwealth Publishers.

Subba, T.B. 1991. *Ethnicity, State and Development: A Case Study of Gorkhaland Movement in Darjeeling,* New Delhi: Vikas Publishing House.

Subba, T.B. 1996. 'Ethnicity, culture and nationalism in North East India: A conspectus'. In M.M. Agarwala (Ed): *Ethnicity, Culture and Nationalism in North East India,* pp. 39-58. New Delhi: Indus Publication.

Tambiah, S. J. 1989. 'Ethnic conflict in the World today'. *American Anthropologists.* May 335-349

Trimble J. E. and R. Dickson. 2005. 'Ethnic gloss'. In C. B. Fisher and R. M. Lerner (Eds): *Applied Developmental Science: An Encyclopaedia of Research, Policies, and Programs.* pp. 412-415. Thousand Oaks: Sage Publishers.

Wilson F. and B. F. Frederiksen. 2000. *Ethnicity, Gender and the Subversion of Nationalism,* London: Frankcass and Co. Ltd. in association with The European Association of Development, Research and Training Institute, Geneva.

8 Genesis of the All India Gurkha League and it's Impact on the Nepalese Identity Movement in Assam

Rudraman Thapa

Under various historical circumstances, the Nepalese of Nepal migrated to different parts of India including Assam at different periods and many of them settled down here permanently[1]. In course of time, despite constituting a substantial number of populations, the Nepalese remained squarely backward and unorganised for long time. As such, there was virtually no Nepali elite organisation in the country till the mid-forties of the last century. The process of mobilising the Nepalese was, however, initiated by a handful of their elite[2] in Darjeeling district of West Bengal, which eventually culminated in the formation of the All India Gurkha League[3] in 1943. Subsequently, it became successful in intensifying organisational base by opening branches in the then provinces particularly in the North East India. In view of this, the present chapter aims at highlighting the genesis of the All India Gurkha League in Darjeeling and its impact on the Nepalese of Assam leading to the formation of the Assam Provincial Gurkha League.

II

Darjeeling, a hilly district of West Bengal, has bulk of its population as Nepalese[4]. According to the first census of 1871-72, the Nepalese formed 34 per cent of total population of Darjeeling district, which rose up to 86 per cent in 1931census[5]. Thus, with the growth of numerical strength and gradual spread of education among the Nepalese in due course, there emerged enlightened elite who realised squarely the backwardness of their community. As a sequence, they became conscious and organised in order to maintain their distinct socio-cultural identity as an effective measure of alleviating overall backwardness. In fact, they wanted to assert socio-political rights for the cause of safeguarding their, what they called, 'legitimate interests'. This became evident when a historic mass meeting was held at Darjeeling on 15th May, 1943 which was presided over by Sardar Bahadur Harjit Dewan Rai while the object of the same was explained by Dambar Singh Gurung who happened to be the chief instrumental agent in inculcating an awareness among the Nepalese and organising them for the cause of preserving distinct self-identity in India. After a prolonged deliberation, the largely attended mass meeting unanimously resolved:

> 'In view of the fact that the condition of the Gurkha spread throughout India is very deplorable and that the political status of the Gurkhas is at stake, an organisation named the All India Gurkha League be formed at this mass meeting of the Gurkhas in order to look after the interests of the Gurkhas in all respects, and particularly, to establish political rights of the Gurkhas in India after the War or whenever any political change takes place in India and further to mobilise the Gurkhas and support the allies in the war efforts[6].

As a result, the All India Gurkha League came into existence with Dambar Singh Gurung[7] as the President and Shiva Kumar Rai as the General Secretary. Further, the mass meeting also formulated and ratified a set of aims and objectives of All India Gurkha League, which were as follows:

(i) To organise and constitute all the Gurkhas spread throughout India and elsewhere into an organic whole;

(ii) To make everyone realise that the Gurkhas belong to the great martial race;

(iii) To preserve the civilisation, tradition and culture of the Gurkhas;

(iv) To further development of Nepali language and create propaganda for its use;

(v) To establish the political rights of the Gurkhas in India;

(vi) To promote friendship and harmony with all the communities in India;

(vii) To have connection with the independent kingdom of Nepal – the mother country of the Gurkhas with devotion and loyalty; and

(viii) To mobilise the Gurkhas spread all over India and to render every possible help specially by supervising manpower to the allies in bringing the world war into speedy and victorious one[8].

III

With the formation of All India Gurkha League, the Nepalese in Darjeeling under its banner began to urge upon the British Government of India to recognise them as a "Separate Minority Community". In support of their demand for the "Separate Minority Community" status, the All India Gurkha League leadership argued that their ancestors had served the British Government in India both in war and peace for generations together and thus they became domicile in India. Moreover, as the Nepalese have a language, culture, tradition and civilisation of their own, they pleaded, that they rightly deserve the status of a Separate Minority Community. Likewise, while substantiating their demand, the All India Gurkha League went on pleading that there are certain numerically smaller communities in India like the Sikhs, the Indian Christians and the Anglo-Indians who had been endowed with the Separate Minority Community status. Thus, while demanding the minority community status for the Nepalese of the country in its first anniversary session held at Darjeeling on 14th May, 1944, the All India Gurkha League resolved:

> Notwithstanding the facts that the British Indian Gurkhas, who are mostly descendants of men that came out of Nepal to serve the Government have been domiciled in India for generations, that they have faithfully served the Governments and the country in "peace and war", that they have their native civilisation, language, culture and tradition, still they have not been recognised as a separate and distinct community; while other smaller communities like the Anglo-Indians who number only 1,40,422 and the Sikhs, the Indian Christians whose population is only equal to that of the Gurkhas, have been recognised as separate communities and provisions have been made for them in the Government of India Act, 1935. This session of All India Gurkha League strongly urges the British Government to recognise this important people as a Separate Minority Community[9].

Since then, the All India Gurkha League went on putting forward a variety of demands before the then British Government of India seeking solution so as to enable them maintain their socio-cultural identity. One of such important demands was the due recognition of Nepali language as vernacular subject of study in educational institutions. Besides, the All India Gurkha League were of the view that since English language is the only medium of answering questions in the Matriculate examination, it became difficult for the Nepali students to excel in the same. On the other hand, while justifying their demand, the Nepali elite pleaded that there are availability of books in Nepali language on various subjects, which might be considerably instrumental in pursuing education for Nepali students. Thus, while pleading for the recognition of Nepali language as a major vernacular subject to be taught and as an medium of University examination, in its first anniversary conference held on 14th May, 1944 at Darjeeling, the All India Gurkha League unanimously resolved:

> The session declares it for a fact that the Nepali language is sufficiently advanced and is spoken by such a large number of people that it be recognised as an important vernacular of India, and as Nepali speaking students are seriously handicapped by being compelled to answer their papers in English in the Matric examination, and as there are sufficient number of books in Nepali on different subjects to meet the requirement of the University curriculum, this session urges the Calcutta University to recognise it as a major vernacular to be taught by the University[10].

It is, however, interesting to note that the All India Gurkha League, at the very inception, developed a conviction that it would not be possible to have overall development of the backward Nepali community unless they enjoy adequate share of power in the decision-making process of the then concerned provinces. In fact, the Nepali elite believed that adequate representation of the Gurkhas in the Central as well as various Provincial Legislatures was indispensable for the cause of dispelling backwardness that might in turn ensure development. Thus, while demanding an amendment to the Government of India Act, 1935 to facilitate the Nepalese to be represented in the Central and various Provincial Legislatures in the first anniversary conference, the All India Gurkha League categorically resolved:

> It is resolved that the British Government be urged to amend the Government of India Act of 1935 as an interim measure before the real Constitution is framed for India so as to enable the Gurkhas to be represented in the Central Legislature and the Provincial Legislatures of the provinces of Assam, Bengal, Bihar, the United Province of Agra and Oudh and the Punjab where the Gurkhas have settled in large numbers[11].

However, despite urging legal safeguards, the Nepali elite also simultaneously held the British Government of India accountable for deliberately keeping the Nepalese of India economically and educationally backward. As such, the All India Gurkha League extended unreserved support to the freedom movement and propagated that only independence of the country from foreign yoke would serve the interest of the Gurkhas best. Furthermore, they joined hands with the local people in opposing the demand for Pakisthan and declared that if necessary thirty lakh *khukris* would be used to defend the unity of the motherland India[12]. Indeed, the Nepalese of the country under the banner of the All India Gurkha League expressed a sense of strong unity and solidarity with the Indians and identified the interest of the country with their own interest as far as the British colonial regime was concerned.

After independence, the Nepali elite of Darjeeling decided to go to the extent of involving into electoral politics under the banner of the All India Gurkha League itself. In fact, the All India Gurkha League leadership, as stated above, was profoundly convinced that adequate share of political power is highly imperative in a bid to safeguard their interests. Such conviction got manifested when in the first general election of 1951-52 to the West Bengal Legislative Assembly, the All India Gurkha League put up their candidate named Shiva Kumar Rai (Jorebunglow constituency), George Manhert (Kurseong Siliguri constituency) and Dal Bahadur Singh (Darjeeling constituency), all of who won the election[13]. Thus, in the subsequent elections also, the All India Gurkha League, used to field its candidates. Largely, the All India Gurkha League got itself converted into a full-fledged political party on the plea to serve the interests of their community.

With the passage of time, the All India Gurkha League, nonetheless, went to the extent of perceiving that mere fighting election and getting a few candidates elected to the Legislative Assembly would not serve their cause adequately. As an alternative strategy, the Nepali elite developed an idea that the interests of the Nepalese could be served best only in a separate Gurkha State. It became reflected when the All India Gurkha League, called upon the people to boycott the mid-term poll of Darjeeling constituency in 1981 in support of their demand for a separate Gurkha State. In this connection, it is worth mentioning that probably taking advantage of people's growing sentiments for a separate Gurkha State, Subhash Ghishing who unsuccessfully contested the Assembly election of 1977 as an independent candidate from Darjeeling constituency[14], subsequently emerged as an undisputed leader of the movement for a separate State viz. Gorkhaland under the banner of the Gurkha National Liberation Front (1981) which began functioning since 1986[15]. Thus, it seems that the emergence of Gurkha National Liberation Front as a "preponderant organisation" has overshadowed the popularity of the All India Gurkha League in Darjeeling largely.

IV

It may, however, be recalled that since its inception, the All India Gurkha League, decided "to organise and consolidate all the Gurkhas spread throughout India and elsewhere into an organic whole". As such, in the event of organising and consolidating the Nepalese, the founding father of All India Gurkha League, Dambar Singh Gurung seemed to be inordinately interested in case of Assam where a large number of the Nepalese were settled permanently. It became evident when in its first annual conference itself held in Darjeeling on 14th May 1944, the All India Gurkha League observed:

> This session agrees entirely with the reported opinion of the special officer appointed by the Government of Assam to enquire whether grazing reserves could be settled that, "the number and areas of grazing reserves is comparatively small and that further reduction would be disastrous to the people, and as almost all the graziers are Gurkhas who did pioneering work to make the land habitable and who have settled in Assam for the last 78 years, this session declares it to be an act of the greatest injustice to attempt to oust the Gurkhas from the land which the suffering and toil of

generations have made habitable by giving settlement of land to the outsiders mainly the *Mussalmans* from Mymensing in Bengal. In view of the report of the special officer, and in view of the fact that cattle is as important as any foodstuff in the shape of meat, milk, butter, cheese etc., this session strongly urges the Government of Assam not to settle grazing land for cultivation purpose[16].

Over and above the then socio-economic plight of the Nepalese in the State, obviously, made it convenient for Dambar Singh Gurung to pay a visit to Assam in the early part of 1944. Mr. Gurung initiated a dialogue with Gopinath Bordoloi, and led a delegation of the Gurkha graziers to Mahammed Sadullah, the then Prime Minister of Assam regarding the problem faced by the Nepali graziers in the Kaziranga forest. The Prime Minister assured him that certain steps would be taken up to look into the matter to evict the illegal Muslim immigrants from the grazing lands[17]. As a result, the Nepalese become so impressed and encouraged by both the All India Gurkha Leagues initiative pertaining to their problems and personal image of Dambar Singh Gurung that they immediately formed the Assam Provincial Gurkha League on August 8, 1944 at Shillong as a State branch of All India Gurkha League[18]. The formation of the only branch of All India Gurkha League in the undivided Assam in turn encouraged Dambar Singh Gurung to pay another visit on January 7, 1945 with a view to organising the Nepalese in the large scale than before for serving the interests of the community. In effect, he had been successful in his mission when under his initiative another branch of the All India Gurkha League was opened on January 9, 1945 at Tezpur[19]. Thus, being influenced by the Nepalese of Darjeeling, the Nepali elite in Assam also began to mobilise their community at regional level so vigorously and effectively that culminated in the opening of good number of branches of the All India Gurkha League, at different places of the State. Some of these branches were at Guwahati (November 11, 1945), Mongoldoi (April 1945), Tinsukia (May 19, 1946), Dibrugarh (June 19, 1946) and Digboi (August 18, 1946)[20]. Mostly the Nepalese of Assam, like their Darjeeling counterparts, increasingly became organised and articulate for maintaining distinct identity as a measure of removing their backwardness. For this purpose, they began to place a variety of demands before the then governments of both the centre and State seeking redressal of grievances, which were more or less similar with All India Gurkha League. Thus, the Assam Provincial Gurkha League became the premier organisation, which virtually initiated the process of mobilising the Nepalese in Assam in collaboration with the All India Gurkha League. In fact, the Assam Provincial Gurkha League gradually became capable of acquiring unprecedented popularity under the leadership of a galaxy of Nepali elite like Charudatta Rai, Sete Rana, Chabilal Upadhyay, Prasad Singh Subba, Dhrubanath Joshi, Dhanraj Subba, Dalbir Singh Lohar, Chabilal Sharma, Kumud Sharma, Karna Singh Chetri, Loknath Joshi, Motilal Chetri, Dalbahadur Chetri, Bishnulal Upadhyay, Gopinarayan Pradhan and many others.

V

Thus, being tremendously influenced by the All India Gurkha League, the Nepali elite of Assam also developed a similar belief that certain constitutional safeguards were indispensable for fulfilling their interests and thereby bringing about development. That is why, by extending full support to the All India Gurkha League's demand for the status of "Minority Community" for the Nepalese, in its first annual conference held at Guwahati on January 1, 1947, the All India Gurkha League resolved:

> The three million Gurkhas though sharing a common tradition with rest of the Indians, nevertheless, have a language, culture and tradition of their own; thus forming a distinct community in India. Hence, this session of the Assam Provincial Gurkha League demands the Constituent Assembly to recognise the Gurkhas statutorily as a Minority Community of India[21].

It may however be recalled that the Nepali leaders of Darjeeling, since the very beginning, realised that unless they get involved into electoral politics, their interests would remain unfulfilled. Such sort of perception became manifested as noted above, when they started fighting election since 1952 under the banner of All India Gurkha League, by turning itself into a full-fledged political party. Such development taking places among the Nepali elite in Darjeeling obviously caused adverse repercussions among the major sections of Nepali elite in Assam. Such adverse reaction compelled the Nepali elite to be dissociated from the AIGL in the year of 1955 on the ground that APGL is not a political organisation. Thus, being dissociated from their Darjeeling counterparts, they categorically declared the APGL, as an apolitical organisation committed to serve their socio-economic interests. More importantly, with the passage of time, the Nepalese of Assam even went to the extent of rechristening the APGL to make it a so-called 'pure socio-cultural organisation'. To this effect, in its 12th Annual Conference held at Gorpal in Darrang district on April 10, 1966 the APGL resolved:

> Assam Pradeshik Gurkha League is purely a social and cultural organisation of the Nepalese of Assam. In keeping with its nature and objectives, this session resolves to bring an amendment in its Article One of its Constitution by changing name, i.e., Assam Pradeshik Gurkha League to Assam Gurkha Sammelon[22].

The change of nomenclature once again evoked sharp reaction within the leadership as well as the regular members of the APGL. Consequently, a tiny section of the Nepali elite such as C.L. Gahatraj, Dhan Bahadur Rai, Sete Rana, Mon Bahadur Subba, Shivaji Rai and many others became, dead against the decision of renaming the APGL, while Prasad Singh Subba, Dalbir Singh Lohar, Lil Bahadur Chetri, Bishnulal Upadhyay etc., fully supported the decision. In effect, the opposition decided to remain as the APGL, whereas the pro-renaming group came out with a newly formed organisation viz. Assam Gurkha Sammelon, more or less, with identical aims and objectives of the former. Thus, the APGL clearly got splitted over the issue of the APGLs involvement into electoral politics and rechristening of nomenclature of the organisation. In course of time, however, the Assam Gurkha Sammelon (hereinafter as the AGS) had been successful in strengthening its organisation capacity as well as popularity compared to APGL that appeared to have lost even its existence. Largely, the AGS emerged as the most articulate monolithic organisation to champion the cause of the Nepalese in Assam.

In spite of getting rechristened as APGL, the isolated form of AIGL, the Nepali elite of Assam, virtually speaking, could not remain completely free from the influence of their Darjeeling counterparts in the event of mobilising their community, especially, on the issues of common interests in the days to come. For instance, being encouraged by the demand seeking the status of the Scheduled Caste and Scheduled

Tribe for a section of the Nepalese of Tibeto-Mongoloid stock in West Bengal and Sikkim, the AGS too put forward the same demand for the entire Nepalese of the State on the ground of overall backwardness. Thus, in a memorandum submitted to the High Powered Committee for the S.C and S.T., Government of India, on July 24, 1968, the AGS pleaded:

> On behalf of the Indian Nepalese, in general and, Nepalese of Assam, in particular, it is requested that due consideration be made for their miserable plight to include the Nepalese as a whole as Scheduled Tribe in the proposed and revised list of Scheduled Castes and Scheduled Tribes of the Constitution so that they may get scope for coming at level of their counterparts in course of time and be able to share the sorrows and happening of the land under the same roof on equal footing with the rest of the citizens of the country[23].

Similarly, on the plea of constitutional right to preserve language and culture, the Nepali elite of Dehradun district of Uttar Pradesh, headed by Anandsingh Thapa, submitted a memorandum to the President of India on January 18, 1956 demanding the inclusion of Nepali language into the Eighth Schedule of Indian Constitution. The linguistic movement of the Nepalese was, however, shifted to Darjeeling when the All India Nepali Bhasa Samiti was formed on January 31, 1972 (hereinafter the AINBS) that spearheaded the movement. The Nepalese in Assam were also not left unaffected by this development and as such extended full support to the linguistic demand of the Nepalese by floating a branch of the AINBS in the same year of inception' i.e., 1972. In view of this, even on the eve of formation of the AINBS, in a memorandum submitted to the Prime Minister of India on January 20, 1972 the AGS argued:

> In the opinion of the eminent linguist like Suniti Kumar Chatterjee, Nepali is one of the fifteen Indian languages. Being in the main lineage of Sanskrit, it is very closely related to Hindi, Bengali, Assamese, Marathi and other languages of Indo Aryan group. We therefore, urge upon your benign self to recognise Nepali language as one of the major languages of India and include it in the Eighth Schedule of the Constitution of India[24].

Thus, the demand for constitutional recognition of Nepali language acquired such a momentum that the Nepalese throughout the country was united for its realisation. It is worthwhile to recall that, the Nepalese in Assam—once declared themselves isolated from the Darjeeling counterparts—now show tremendous enthusiasm by participating in all phases of the movement led by Darjeeling-based organisations such as AIGL, AINBS, and Bharatiya Nepali Rastriya Parishad, etc. They also submitted memorandum to the Government of India as well as Assam for considerable times passed resolutions in every annual conference demanding inclusion of Nepali language into the Constitution. The linguistic sentiment made the Nepalese of the State so determined and pledged, that a section of them reportedly went to the extent of forming 'suicide squad' in 1992 for this cause[25]. In fact, it became possible on the part of the Nepali elite of Assam to be so successful in mobilising their community only with the help of the Darjeeling counterparts even by forgetting their erstwhile disassociation. In addition to the AGS; the APGL; the All Assam Nepali Students Union; Nepali Sahitya Parishad, Assam; Nawadhwani Sangathan, etc. were also equally concerned about the linguistic demand and took steps from time to time to realise the same. It would not be, therefore, an exaggeration to say that in the event of mobilising their community the Nepali elite of Assam were influenced and would be influenced by their Darjeeling counterparts for all times to come[26].

VI

It may however be reiterated that the dominant section of the Nepali elite categorically characterised the AGS as a 'pure socio-cultural organisation' in 1966. Indeed, they seemed to be superficially desired to keep the AGS aloof from power politics and reported it to be the focal point as why the Nepalese in Assam got themselves delinked from Darjeeling counterparts. Despite so, it is surprising to note that even before their dissociation from the AIGL, the Nepali elite of Assam, like the Darjeeling counterparts, were also convinced that the adequate share of political power was essential for safeguarding their interests. As such, they used the AGS (formerly APGL) as a political platform to build up their political career and bargain with rural elite for adequate share of power in the decision-making process of the State. For instance, on the eve of the first general election in one of its meetings of the Executive

Committee held at Singri of Darjeeling district on July 26, 1951, the then APGL (now the AGS) unanimously adopted a resolution demanding twelve electoral constituencies to be reserved by the Assam Provincial Congress Committee (APCC) for the Nepalese[27]. Similarly, they went on claiming adequate representation of the Nepalese in the Assam Legislative Assembly. For this reason, in its Tenth Annual Conference held at Lanka of Nagaon district on April 20, 1961 the, APGL strongly resolved:

> Whereas the Gurkhas of Assam have not so far been satisfactorily represented in the State Legislature, and whereas having completely identified themselves with the interest of Assam, they have been considerably contributing to the progress, prosperity and security of the State, this tenth session of the Assam Pradeshik Gurkha League resolves that the Assam Pradesh Congress Committee be requested to give nomination to the Gurkha Congressmen from the following constituencies: (i) Digboi, (ii) Gohpur and (iii) Bodsola[28].

In this way, under the banner of the AGS, the Nepali elite used to recommend name of Nepali members to be nominated by the APCC as its candidate in each general election. Considering their growing numerical strength, the APCC also used to nominate a few Nepali leaders as its nominees in election who generally got elected. In due course, however, the prospect of getting the Congress nomination depended on the personal capacity of the Nepali leaders to mobilise their community so as to occupy a key position in the AGS. It became a tradition ever since the APCC started nominating those Nepali leaders who were holding top offices in the AGS. Perhaps for this reason, Dalbir Singh Lohar, Bishnulal Upadhaya, Chandra Bahadur Chetri, Kul Bahadur Chetri, Padam Bahadur Chauhan, Moni Kumar Subba, Rudra Parajuli, Tanka Bahadur Rai became successful in getting elected to the ALA as the Congress nominee since they happened to be the prominent office bearers of the AGS. Currently, there are two Nepali leaders of whom one is elected to the Parliament, named Moni Kumar Subba while another named Tanka Bahadur Rai, both elected to the ALA as the Congress (I) nominees who are simultaneously holding the office of the President and General Secretary of the AGS respectively. Indeed, major section of the AGS leaders happened to be out and out

Congressmen, and therefore, it is quite obvious that the AGS is used as the Congress (I) platform to serve the interests of the Nepali community. Under such circumstances, the AGS once even went to the extent of demanding a berth for the Nepalese in the Council of Minister of Assam. As such, in a memorandum submitted to the Chief Minister of Assam on April 22, 1972, the AGS pleaded:

> Although the work of ministry formation is over, it has come to our sight through press report that is going to be expanded very soon. Like all the minority groups here, the Nepalese have also a sizeable population in Assam. Some of whom are in defence service and others engaged in agriculture and labour in far- flung areas doing their best for defence and production of the country. They will feel proud and secure even after 25 years of long Congress rule if C.B.Chetri – the only representative of this community in the Legislature is taken in the Cabinet. We are confident that Shri Chetri being quite young, educated and active can shoulder the responsibility of administration under your able guidance[29].

Perhaps, considering such plea of the Nepalese for the first time, Kul Bahadur Chetri, a former Nepali leader of the AGS was inducted into the Council of Ministers of Assam (1991-1996) headed by Sri Hiteswar Saikia with a portfolio of Cabinet rank in 1991. Similarly, Tanka Bahadur Rai, another Congress (I) Nepali MLA, has been recently elected as the Deputy Speaker of the Assam Legislative Assembly. Indeed, the major section of the Nepali elite seemed to be politically ambitious, and hence, capitalised their organisation and symbol in bid to fulfil the political aspirations of the community. Therefore, in order to have adequate share of political power, the mobilisation of the Nepalese appeared to their elite as absolutely essential to gain for their community. In spite of so, it is not unnatural that sometimes individual interests got precedence over the interests of the community as a whole. Nonetheless, it is obvious that the Nepali elite under the banner of the AGS are consciously or unconsciously getting involved into the game of power politics for, what they call community development.

VII

From the above discourse, it is evident that the process of mobilising the Nepalese first started in Darjeeling under the stewardship of Dambar

Singh Gurung that culminated in the formation of AIGL. The Nepali elite of Darjeeling well realised that the maintenance of distinct identity of the Nepalese in India was essential as a measure of alleviating their overall backwardness. The AIGL leadership, therefore, demanded the recognition of Nepalese as a Separate Minority Community, recognition and introduction of Nepali language as a vernacular subject of study in educational institutions, etc. At the same time, they perceived that without having adequate share of political power, the interests of Nepalese could not be protected. They, therefore, urged upon the dominant political authority to make provision for the adequate representation of the Nepalese in the law-making bodies. After independence however, a significant breakthrough took place in the AIGL when it turned itself into a political party and began to contest elections as a means of ventilating grievances effectively in the Legislature to bring about development of the Nepali community.

The formation of AIGL and its growing activities greatly influenced the Nepalese of Assam, which eventually led to them to float the APGL. Under the banner of APGL (renamed as the AGS), the Nepalese of the State worked in collaboration with its parent organisation i.e. AIGL for quite a long time. However, they gave up their co-relationship with the AIGL on the ground that it got involved into the game of power politics. Interestingly, despite doing so, it appeared that the Nepalese in Assam used to identify their movement with Darjeeling, particularly on the issues of common interest, such as, the movement for the inclusion of Nepali language into the Constitution of India, inclusion of the Nepalese into the S.C and S.T lists, etc. Of late, the Gurkhaland movement also reportedly made certain degree of impact on the Nepalese in Assam. Over and above, while raising any demand, the Nepalese used to refer the case of West Bengal and Sikkim such as the demand for the status of the Scheduled Caste and Scheduled Tribe in order to justify their claims. In fact, they could not make themselves as free from the influence of Darjeeling counterparts as desired; rather, the latter acted as a great source of impetus for the former.

Furthermore, what is striking to note is that despite characterising the AGS as a non-political organisation, politically ambitious section of the Nepali elite used it as a Congress (I) political platform in order to elect representatives for ventilating their grievances in the Assam

Legislative Assembly. More importantly, the politically ambitious Nepali leaders and even the sitting Nepali Congress members of the Assam Legislative Assembly happened to be the top office bearers of the AGS– a so-called 'pure socio-cultural organisation' of the Nepalese. Thus, it appeared to the Nepali elite that the mobilisation of the community under the banner of the AGS to protect interests was essential to bargain with the ruling elite for adequate share of political power. In fact, the emerging Nepali elite are rightly or wrongly getting involved into the game of power politics on the pretext of serving the community. However, it is an undeniable fact that the politics of mobilisation of the Nepalese in Assam could best be understood in the context of the Nepalese of Darjeeling and their movement for distinct identity as a measure of protecting interests.

Notes and References

1. By the mid 20th century, one in every 10 Nepalese had emigrated. In India alone, by 1970, there were 1.5 million number, out of a population of 11.55 million in Nepal. The annual rate of migration in 1961 was 82,000 a year, 20,000 of whom remained in India permanently each year. Even in 1900, over 250,000 Nepalese – one in every 20 were already living in North India. (See D.C.Upadhyay and Jose Cl. Abneva, 1975, *Population and Development in Nepal, Kathmandu*, and cited in Smikant Dutta, 1981, 'Migration and Development: The Nepalese in North East', *Economic and Political Weekly*, Mumbai, June 13, 1981).

2. A handful of Nepali elite of Darjeeling district includes Sardar Bahadur Hanjit Dewan Rai, Dambar Singh Gurung, Rup Narayan Sinha, Shiva Kumar Rai, Randhir Subba, Ari Bahadur Gurung, Jangbir Thapa, George Manhert and many others.

3. In this connection, it is worth mentioning that under the leadership of Thakur Chandan Singh, a retired Indian army, another All India Gurkha League was established at Dehradun of Uttar Pradesh (now Uttaranchal) in 1921. A new branch of the League was also opened at Dibrugarh in Assam in 1927. Ananta Lal Sharma, a Nepali resident of Assam was even sentenced for trying to enlist local Gurkha soldiers in Civil Disobedience Movement (see Kanchanmoy Mazumdar, *Nepal and Indian Nationalist Movement,* Calcutta 1975, pp. 27-34).

4. There has been an unending controversy regarding the nomenclature among the inhabitants of Darjeeling district. The Gurkha National Liberation Front led by Subhash Ghising adamantly stick to identify themselves as the 'Gurkhas' and not as the 'Nepalese'. They claim that

'Gorkha' means a Nepali speaking Indian National while Nepalese means Nepali-speaking national of Nepal. In view of this, in the present chapter the words 'Nepalese' and 'Gurkhas' are interchangeably used to mean the same people in the context of India.

5. See 'Language of Neglect: The Nepali Question'. *Frontier*, February 29, 1992, pp 8, and also see Tanka Bahadur Subba, *Dynamics of a Hill Society: The Nepalese in Darjeeling and Sikkim Himalayas*, 1989, New Delhi, Mittal Publications, p. 14.

6. Bhai Nahar Singh and Kirpal Singh, 1987, *History of All India Gurkha League, 1943-1949*. New Delhi, Nirmal Publishers and Distributors, p. 3.

7. Mention may be made that Dambar Singh Gurung was the first Nepali MLA who was elected to the Bengal Legislative Assembly in 1937. Again, in 1945 elections to the Bengal Legislative Assembly, Gurung was elected for the second time as the AIGL nominee supported by the Indian National Congress. Besides, he happened to be a member of the Constituent Assembly (Lil Bahadur Kshetri, *Dambar Singh Gurung: Sangkhipta Parichay Smritigrantha,* 22nd Biennial Conference of the AGS, Guwahati 22nd May, 1997, pp 2 – 3).

8. Op. cit., p. 54

9. Op. cit., pp. 25-26.

10. Op. cit., p. 27.

11. Op. cit., p. 26.

12. A.C. Bhuyan and S.P.De, 1980, *Political History of Assam*, 1940-1947, Volume II, Government of Assam, Dishpur, June 1980, pp. 317-318.

13. Chiranjib Kumar Kar, 1991, *Sub-Regional Movement in India: A Study of Political History of the Gurkhas of Darjeeling District, Calcutta*, Firma KLM Pvt. Ltd., pp. 41-42.

14. Chiranjib Kumar Kar, *ibid.,* pp. 41-42.

15. It may be noticed that ever since the formation of GNLF (right from 1980), Subhash Ghising travelled from village to village with a slogan that the Nepalese should preserve their identity. His contention was that they are Nepalese first and belonged to CPI (M) or Congress next. He tried to boycott the 1984 general election by saying 'no State, no Vote' but he was completely ignored. The expulsion of Nepalese from Meghalaya compelled the Nepalese of Darjeeling to ponder the demand of Subhash Ghising. Thus, Subhash Ghising became the champion of Nepalese in the hills of West Bengal (See Suman Raj Timsina, 1992,

Nepali Community in India, Delhi, Manik Publications Pvt. Ltd. pp. 48-49).

16. Resolution passed in the open session of the First Anniversary of the All India Gurkha League held at Darjeeling on May 14 1944, cited in Bhai Nahar Singh and Kirpal Singh, 1987, *ibid*, p. 26.

17. Gurkha' (Nepali Fortnightly) Guwahati, January 1, 1945, cited in Bhuyan and De, *op.cit.*, pp. 318-319.

18. Bhai Nahar Singh and Kirpal Singh, *op. cit*, p. 52.

19. According to another source, 'in 1944, the first branch of All India Gurkha League was opened at Tezpur and Prasad Singh Subba was President of this branch' (See Purushottam Bhandari, 1996, *Freedom Movement and Role of Indian Nepalese*, 1800-1950. Jagiroad, Assam, p. 68).

20. A short note on the All India Gurkha League and its branches in Assam cited in Bhai Nahar Singh and Kirpal Singh, *op.cit.*, pp. 51-52.

21. Resolution of the Assam Provincial Gurkha League adopted in the first Annual Conference held at Guwahati on December 31, 1946 and January 1, 1947.

22. Resolution adopted in the 12th Conference of the Assam Provincial Gurkha League held at Gorpal of Darrang district on April 10, 1966.

23. Memorandum of the AGS submitted to the Government of India on July 24, 1968.

24. Memorandum of the AGS submitted to the Prime Minister of India, New Delhi on January 20, 1972.

25. Reported in the *Agradoot* (Assamese bi-weekly), Guwahati, November 8, 1992.

26. It is worth noting that on the eve of giving constitutional recognition to Nepali language, a section of politically ambitious Nepalese under the leadership of Subhash Ghising, Chairman, Darjeeling Gurkhaland Hill Council, vehemently opposed the proposal of the Government of India to include 'Nepali Language' into the Constitution. Mr. Ghising demanded the inclusion of 'Gorkhali language' in lieu of 'Nepali', which he termed as a foreign language. The other section of the Nepalese led by Nar Bahadur Bhandari, former Chief Minister of Sikkim pleaded for the inclusion of 'Nepali Language' recognised by the Sahitya Academy instead of 'Gorkhali'. He was of strong opinion that Nepali and Gorkhali are virtually the one and same language. The vocabulary conflict of this kind did not leave the Nepalese of Assam also unaffected. A section pleaded for 'Gorkhali Language', while the other section advocated for

'Nepali Language'. Nevertheless, 'Nepali Language' got precedence over Gorkhali in the long run and was included in the Constitution of India on August 20, 1992.

27. Bishnulal Upadhyay, 1984, *Assamay Nepaliharu* (in Nepali), Tezpur, p. 20.

28. Resolution adopted by the APGL in the 10th Annual Conference held at Lanka of Nagaon district on April 10, 1961.

29. Memorandum of the AGS submitted to the Chief Minister of Assam on April 22, 1972.

9 The Problem of Ethnicity: Some Observations with Reference to Manipur in North East India

Rajat Kanti Das

Though ethnicity has many dimensions, ethnic self-consciousness remains central to it, which manifests itself either in the demand for cultural survival or for political sovereignty. Ethnic consciousness is the cementing factor behind social solidarity lying at the root of social action and political action at a given moment of time. Within the liberal socio-anthropological tradition, ethnic phenomena have now occupied an important place in the process of social formation.

In this chapter, an attempt has been made to focus on such manifestations of ethnicity as may be indicative of ethnic identity. This necessarily calls for underlining ethnic group-specific features. The basic assumption here is that, ethnicity in the form of ethnic differences or ethnic group specifically, account for differential expression of identity. In the contemporary situation, the question of ethnic group identity has assumed central significance. This has become a problem area today. Although it has become a global phenomenon, the question needs to be examined in a regional perspective since the ethnic groups function in a specific regional context.

It may be profitable to examine the situation prevailing in Manipur in North East India, where two tribal groups have been involved in a bitter, violent conflict to assert their own ethnic identity. The Naga-Kuki conflict is the best example of that. One has to concede that political conflict reflecting the problem of ethnic identity does not follow the same course everywhere. In North East India, conflict sometimes takes the form of an open ethnic violence. In the Naga-Kuki conflict, two ethnic groups are directly involved, who have been trying to project their respective identities through armed struggle without the intervention of any political party. In this situation, most of the societal roles take the form of political roles and the whole community functions more like a political community. The third element in this conflict is the government, either in the form of the State government with the police force at its command, or the Central government deploying an army in this armed conflict, sometimes taking sides for strategic reasons.

II

In recent times, insurgent violence in almost the whole of North East has turned this verdant, sub-Himalayan region into a virtual killing field. It appears that the underground outfits operate here with near impunity. On the other side, the escalating violence is also attributed to counter insurgency operations undertaken by the security men. There were quite a number of incidents where the direct involvement of the Government controlled Army had further intensified the conflict. The predicament of the Maring villagers after the June 29, 1993 operation in which a group of NSCN (National Socialist Council of Nagaland) members ambushed an Army convoy on the Pallel-Moreh segment in the Chandel district of Manipur is worth pointing out. In the said operation, twenty-two army personnel, two of them commissioned officers, had been killed and the NSCN claimed to have captured a sizeable amount of arms and ammunition from the ambushed Army at the expense of life of two guerrillas. In a press communique issued by the information and publicity cell of the 'Government of the People's Republic of Nagaland' later, the NSCN also claimed that at least four Kuki militants travelling with the Army convoy had also been killed but denied Army claims that one Captain Johnny, a NSCN rebel, was among the casualties. Among other things, the whole incidents points at the Army's rather soft attitude towards the Kukis. The repeated claims made by the Maring villagers that there villagers would first be searched by the Army personnel, who on occasions used arms, to be inevitably followed by Kuki militant raids, also hint at the possibility of a secret understanding between the Army and Kuki militants. Incidentally, in the Tengnaupal T.D. Block, where the Maring population is mainly concentrated, there are Thadou villages in some areas. One such village is Sita, which also came under attack from Naga militants on a few occasions. The village has since then come under Army protection. It needs to be pointed out here that the Marings have Naga affiliation and there have been stories of their direct conflict with the Thadou Kukis in the past. Maring personalities like Angtisan, Kottisan have been raised to the stature of national heroes because they could successfully fight the Kukis and became victorious. The Naga-Kuki clash, which has been going on since mid-1992, has cost both sides dearly. Many have been killed and thousands of Nagas and Kukis have lost their houses, villages and vocations. Ironically, the Government of Manipur attributed the genesis of the clashes to rivalry between Naga and Kuki timber merchants who smuggle teak across the borders from Myanmar and the refusal to pay "taxes" to the NSCN. This is one-way of justifying the validity of the insurgent group. It no longer remains a mere insurgent group, whose viability at the political level can be dismissed outright.

That the conflict is not a sudden development needs no confirmation. It is probably the culmination of a long process of polarisation of ethnic sentiments and aggrandisation of forces acting upon them. The use of the term "Kuki" is not without controversy and contradiction. John Shakespear (1912) wrote: "The term Kuki is not recognised by the people to whom it is applied". The first reference of the Kukis was probably made in 1777 A.D., when these tribesmen attacked the British subjects in the Chittagong Hill tracts when Warren Hastings was the Governor General of Bengal. The British administrator who had a hazy knowledge about them rather arbitrarily applied the term to them. The British Government did not have the opportunity of direct administration in Manipur and adjoining areas before 1891. It has been suggested that Maharaja Nara Singh settled the Kuki migrants of the eighteenth century in the Manipur hills with the assistance of the British Political Agent W. McCulloch. The Kuki irregulars were reported to have formed a part of the standing Army of the State before 1891. The British invented the term "Old Kuki" to be differentiated from the later Kuki migrants (New Kukis – represented by the Thadous), and it was applied to the Manipur tribes, which had linguistic affinity with the Kukis. The affinity of the so-called Old Kuki tribes needs further scrutiny. Tribes like Moyon, Monshang and Lamgang have a long history of settlement in Manipur. Tarao, Aimol, Chiru, Chothe were all tribute-paying tribes in the twelfth century as indicated in old historical documents (*Loyamba shilyen,* for example). Today, some of such tribes are more attracted towards the Naga ideology. Some have even accepted the Naga identity. Tribes like Anal, Aimol, Moyon, Monshang, Lamgang, Tarao, Chothe, and Chiru also functioned as 'bridge and buffer communities' between the Naga and those Kuki Chins who had accepted the Naga identity. The British Government also used the Thadous as a 'buffer' between two sections of warring Naga groups. One may like to trace the source of the present conflict to the British policy of using the Kukis, particularly the later migrants, as a 'buffer' community. Nevertheless, at the same time it has also to be conceded that the Nagas themselves were not very much averse to Kuki presence in their midst. One reason could be that the Kukis never posed any threat to undermining Naga political domination. Rarely did they go against Naga political control in Naga-dominated areas. British colonialism was also to some extent responsible for generating the Naga national feeling. Even the Meitei king could not bring the powerful Naga tribes like the Tangkhul, Mao under their control. Today, at the political level both the Naga and the Kuki extremists are equally firm and unrelenting in their demand for an independent Nagaland and Kukiland. Even the State political leaders are involved in the process in some way or the other. The gunning down of Mr. Chungkhokai Doungel, the ex-Finance Minister and a Kuki leader, sometime back at the heart of Imphal town by the suspected NSCN guerrillas bears testimony of that.

III

While the Nagas, in general, fulfil the conditions of an ethnic group, the same cannot be said about the Kukis. The Kuki identity has been developed, pursued and propagated by the Thadous. They mainly organise interaction among the members of the group. The Kuki National Army is not only their creation; the recruits largely come from them. Be it Nagas or Kukis, 'culture-bearing' functions of the respective ethnic groups have been exaggerated to give an impression of exclusiveness. Undoubtedly, the primary objective of both the groups is to create 'corporate political followings' to sustain the armed struggle. At the ethnic group level, the collective *we* feeling is essential for developing a pattern of social interaction. The type of ethnic group representation by the Nagas or Kukis is not confined to the level of a single community. There are difficulties in applying the notion of a 'people' here. The notion of a 'people' in the sense of a large group of broadly similar and related individuals and greater in size than individual community groups is in itself dependent upon the existence in the world of large political units. In the present situation, the unifying nature of the tribe can be maintained only if it functions as a political unit. However, where a constellation of tribes is involved sharing a common ethnic identity, the emergence of a higher order polity is probably the precondition. It also envisages a situation where there is a proper linkage or a level of integration between social interaction and political culture. The term 'polity' is used to identify an aggregate with a common set of corporate forms. In one sense, polity refers to the society of which this is the political form. As a form of political organisation, a polity represents the political aspects of society. The polity coincides in its form and limits with the maximum spread of the social institutional framework within which power and authority are distributed and public regulation proceeds. Therefore, when we speak of Naga or Kuki polity, we are in reality thinking about a type of society functioning as a political unit.

IV

The functioning of political variables assumes a greater significance when looked as a manifestation of ethnicity. Ethnicity in the form of ethnic differences has to be considered in the light of specific socio-political situation. From another consideration, ethnic differences seem to be directly associated with variations in power and material wealth.

> "Groups of equal power may mutually enforce principles of closure their members keep separate from each other, but neither group dominates the other" Giddens, 1989.

Probably, the Nagas and Kukis have reached a point of closure at present, and this may be because of the fact that the Nagas today are not in a position to dominate over the Kukis. In other words, the Kukis are making their presence increasingly felt in the field of power. On Sunday, the 6th October 1996, the following news item appeared in the Telegraph:

> "Kuki rebels kill two Assam Rifles men".

This is significant in view of the fact that the Kukis could take up the role previously monopolised by the Nagas. Militants of the Kuki

National Army (KNA) are originally, a Myanmar-based group, who have now been trying to shift its base to Manipur after the Naga-Kuki clashes erupted. Now, they are to some extent successful in doing that. In another report in the same issue of the paper, one could know about the mounting tension in Makui Naga village and its surrounding areas after violent clashes between Naga and Kuki militants continued for two weeks. Makui, a Liangmei Naga village about 100 km. from Imphal, is situated inside the Kanglatombi forest reserve in Senapati district's trouble-torn Sadar Hills sub-division. The whole area became the source of conflicting tension ever since the Government's decision to create a separate Sadar Hills district where the Kukis outnumber the Naga population. Incidents of inter-community clashes took place after that. The question of Naga-Kuki conflict has to be seen under specific historical circumstances. The level of social consciousness and cultural specificity displayed by the Nagas or Kukis will be at variance with strategic action for group solidarity to be used for mastering greater power in the political field. Both the groups are aspiring for a political identity bearing the stamp of cultural specificity, and it is this convergence of interests that has probably brought them into sharp conflict with one another. By taking recourse to conflict, the two groups are, in fact, trying to maintain ethnic distinctiveness. "Self-conception" is at the very root of ethnic identity, where 'self' is identified with the 'group' to which one belongs. Admittedly, a greater degree of inter-ethnic interaction tends to reduce conflicting tendencies shown by one ethnic group towards the other. Epstein (1978), analyses the process of 'self-conception' taking a cue from Leach. The process emphasises more on projecting the self and consequently, one's own group. It may be paraphrased in the following way:

> "If I am I, simply because I am I, and thou art thou simply because thou art thou, then I am I and thou art thou. But if I am I because thou art thou, and thou art thou because I am I, then I am not I and thou art not thou".

One has a feeling that, in the present situation, self-projection and in-group sentiments has been overplayed reaching a point of exaggeration.

Today, inter-ethnic link between the Nagas and Kukis in the form of marital tie, associational tie or participation in joint economic ventures is hardly encouraged. The Naga-Kuki conflict points to the deliberate creation of self-consciousness by the competing groups to promote and protect their own ethnic identity, which has political implications in the form of empowerment of the concerned people.

Some of the recent happenings now direct the attention to the fast deteriorating relation between the Meiteis and Kukis. A bitter conflict has erupted between the two communities cantering on Mayanmar border town of Moreh. Moreh has now become 'a veritable ethnic powder keg'. It all started with militants mowing down 12 people on June 9, 2007. Before that, on June 3, unidentified gunmen killed a Meitei auto rickshaw driver in the heart of Moreh market. A *bandh* was called by several local organisations and a demand was made to remove the Assam Rifles unit from the area on the ground that it is trying to create a rift between the Meiteis and Kukis by colluding with the killers. It was further alleged that the Army was responsible for killing many innocents. The UNLF, meanwhile, has made its position clear by saying that, though there is as such no rivalry with the Kukis, it will not spare them and deal with them firmly if they allow themselves to be used by the Indian Army as their agents. However, reports in the *Imphal Free Press* (quoted by I. Lama in the *Statesman,* June 18, 2007) suggest the involvement of the militant outfit, in all probability, the United National Liberation Front, who had killed five Kuki National Army / Kuki National Organisation members, and inflamed Kukis from a Meitei locality, killing five workers from Imphal. Tensions between the two communities have been simmering over the past few months. Some 300 villagers in Chandel district bordering Myanmar were reported to have fled to seek shelter in Moreh; many more were interrupted and turned back. There was another report of the alleged "abduction" of 400 Kukis from T. Lijang to Myanmar by UNLF and Myanmarese junta personnel, which was of course promptly denied by the Meitei underground outfit. However, the Kukis did not change their stand and squarely blamed the UNLF for turning Chandel into a battlefield.

Of late, Moreh has become the centre of much entrepreneurial activities as not only are the interests of Kukis and other smaller tribal communities involved, but also those of Meities and Tamils are closely entangled. At the top of it, the underground organisation like UNLF,

Kuki National Army and Kuki National Organisation are bent upon gaining control over the business, which holds much promise. The observations made by I. B. Lama seem to be relevant here.

> .... unrest in Moreh is bound to dampen entrepreneurial enthusiasm. As it is, Indo-Myanmarese trade, which opened in April 1995, is yet to pick up, with frequent blockades of the crucial national highways, not to forget the rampant extortion by various vested interests. The Centre has sanctioned Rs.70 crores for the construction of modern trade infrastructure to match that of Myanmarese and other South Eastern countries and it also plans to hold an international trade fair at Moreh.
>
> But the problem is obvious; ethnic groups are vying for control of the lucrative Moreh market, now in the hands of Tamils who settled there ....after Myanmar deported them in the early 1960s.
>
> Kukis and Meiteis lived in peace for generations and the current alarming turnaround is certainly the handiwork of those bent on profit. (I. B. Lama, *The Statesman*, 18th June, 2007).

There is no denying the fact that the underground organisations have all along been striving to derive political mileage by trying to control economic profit-making activities. In this case, political objective remains hidden unlike the one represented by the Naga-Kuki conflict. The more, people of different ethnic group character come together at the economic front, the more they are concerned with remaining distinctive to create a political space for themselves. However, this applies to communities operating along ethnic line to control resources. Broadly speaking, when resources are no longer in sole control of ethnic groups, ethnicity has more and more pervaded the field of politics.

References

Barth, F. 1969. *Ethnic Groups and Boundaries: The Social Organization of Culture Differences.* London: Allen and Unwin.

Giddens, A. 1989. *Sociology.* Cambridge: Polity Press.

Lama, I. B. 2007. 'The North East of Eden'. *The Statesman*, Monday, June 18.

Okley, J. and H. Callaway. 1991. *Anthropology and Autobiography.* ASA Monograph 29: Routeledge.

Sanajaoba, N. 1995. *Manipur : Past and Present.* New Delhi: Mittal Publications.

10 Supra Tribalism: Search for a New Way in Manipur

M.C. Arun

The question of ethnicity and tribalism has not been discussed in India vis-a-vis the nationhood and nation-building; rather the question of tribal life and their exploitation have been focused mainly from the human rights perspectives, tribal development or Elwinian romanticism. Without having a definition of 'tribe' in the Constitution of India, several economic, social and developmental debates are in the air. The notion of tribe and their condition is, even, not uniform in the national psyche. Hence, the academic or political discourses on the tribal and tribalism are not uniformly perceived in India. Moreover, the tribal way of life is still considered as what the colonial writers projected. The changes in these 'tribal societies' that have been occurred in the post-colonial period are not fully understood within a national framework. This results into adhoc arrangements in fighting tribal unrest or revolts. Where is or should be tribal position in a nation? And should they still be considered as having tribal sovereignty? Is nation a conglomeration of several 'sovereign' entities? These questions are a few; many more questions can be raised up in 'tribal-nation' relationship.

Ted Liu (2012), in his thought-provoking article, opens up an issue about the ethnic minorities in the context of Arab that, in spite of elections and constitutional reforms, the political integration of tribal and ethnic minorities in several countries with majority Arab populations remains incomplete. In some countries, tribes are influential and are a part of the established political landscape, but in others, they remain marginalised and survive on the economic and political fringe (Liu, 2012). Likewise, in India, the tribal relations with the majority people and their position in social and political landscape are not uniform. Hence, any move towards democratisation in tribal society brings different results. The experiences in tribal areas of North East India are not similar with that of Andaman or of Central India. Even in the North East India, the ethnic politics in each State has unique history and uniqueness about each of them. Further, Ted Liu opines that, *if the leadership ensures a politically inclusive process and strikes a balance between national unity and regional autonomy; ethnic diversity need not be an obstacle to democratisation.* If it is true, then why does democratisation in tribal areas always bring a chaotic situation in India, especially in North East India? The political havocs around the issues of Autonomous District Councils are more or less common in all the States in North East India. The nature of Indian rule in India's tribal areas could not negotiate with the ethnic politics. Unlike India, we could see Post-apartheid South Africa's successfully transition from white minority rule to multi-party democracy in which the country's numerous ethnic groups were properly represented. Potential barriers to national unity such as Zulu and Afrikaner nationalism were successfully negotiated (Liu, 2012). In this line of thought, we can see of India's failure in making a nation and in handling tribal interests or politics. In short, India still does not know how to integrate the tribal peoples in its national framework.

The dialectics of tribalism and detribalisation requires to be focused in order to understand the emerging or well stabilised tribal politics in India, especially in North East India. Both the processes are neutral to the nationalism. Still there is a question whether these processes have a serious potential threat to the same nationalism or whether both the processes lead to a new National frame, independent of the existing nation.

To understand the term 'tribalism', we can look into the four meanings given by D H Reader (Reader, 1970):

1. The state of living in tribes: a generic sense, to which the name tribalism may be given. The quality of living in tribes is *tribal.*
2. Remaining in, keeping in contact with, or returning to settle in tribal areas. This sociographic sense, often in the context of migration, may be called *ruralism.* The adjective would be rural-tied, the transition *ruralised.*

3. Adherence to tribal values and behavior patterns. This psycho-sociological dimension may be relevant in town or country, and in view of common usage will be called "tribalism" (in quotation marks). The transitional condition is *"tribalisation,"* the adjective *"tribalised."*
4. A category of interaction among Africans in towns. Research in Central Africa (e.g., Epstein, 1956: 724; Mitchell, 1956a: 18) has appropriated the generic term tribalism to this context. Actually, a role-category is involved which will be designated here as tribe. The adjective, if needed, is *tribe-categorised* (emphasis original).

All the senses are embodied in the term 'tribalism'. In a more political sense, more in political anthropological studies of tribal politics within contemporary national framework, tribalism is manifested in a complex manner. In North East India, we observe a peculiar combination of tribalism and combination. The members of a particular 'tribe' may show (a) tribalism in urban setting and detribalisation in rural population as well as (b) tribalism in a rural context and detribalisation in urban context. The adherence to their original tribal villages of the urban tribal groups is seen because of their land security in the village which is much linked with their kinship affiliations, kinship relationships, etc. In African setting, similar studies had been done by various anthropologists, such as Watson, Gluckman. Watson points out that, in Zambia, land is still the final tribal security. As long as rights to the use of land continue to depend on kinship affiliations, kin relationships will retain their importance. Gluckman, similarly, states that those who stay at home hold the land as security for support in money from those who go out to work (Reader, 1970).

India is confused with what a tribe is. In 19th century literatures, the term tribe is used to mean a form of social organisation based on kinship and locality. Tribesmen usually, as assumed, consider themselves descendants of a common ancestor. In other words, a tribe is thought to be a group of people who are descended from common ancestors and ruled by a hereditary chief, who share a single culture (including, in particular, language and religion), and who live in a well-defined geographical region (Paglia, 2008). This is not always true. This concept of tribe is no more relevant in modern usage. Moreover, an individual or a community may have a tribal identity, but live within a corresponding tribal structure or adhere to norms of tribal culture. For example, in the US, there are many Americans who identify themselves as Cherokee, or part-Cherokee, but have no experience with Cherokee tribal structure or culture (Munoz, 2010). In India, the Constitution does not define the term tribe though tribal provisions are given under several provisions and schedules. This kind of confusion at national level makes more chaotic and confusing states of affairs in the States.

In Manipur, as a part of safeguarding tribal rights, the tribal lands are kept outside the purview of Manipur Land Reforms and Land Revenue Act, 1960. Moreover, the colonial administration divided the State into two distinct administrative zones on topographical basis: the Hill and the Plain. There is still legacy of colonialism in State administration of Manipur. The tribal villages enjoy autonomy vis-à-vis land laws which govern ownership, distribution, and rights in land. Under Kuki land laws, the chief is one having absolute power in land. He is the supreme authority in the village affairs. He owns the entire land within his jurisdiction. There is neither clan land nor individual. He distributes land for cultivation and plot for dwelling house construction. The Kuki chief has the authority to expel any villager from the village. Villagers live at the pleasure of the chief. The Kuki administration is autocratic and the chief is the autocrat (Daimai, 2011). It may be recalled that after the Kuki rebellion of 1917-19, the Kuki chiefs enjoyed a special position in colonial administration.

In other tribal areas such as that of the Tangkhul, Rongmeis, Mao, the land belongs to village authority. Plots of land are distributed by the Village chiefs in Councils. The land distributions are done on the basis of lineage, clan and kin groups. There is a portion of land that belongs to the village.

However, it is true to all the tribal villages in Manipur that individual persons have no permanent rights in land; their rights are adhered with their belonging to the villages, kin relationships. This fact is the basis of tribal cohesion of urban tribal groups to their original villages and their obligation to their kin groups who are living in their original villages. On the other hand, the urban tribal peoples are well exposed to the urban amenities, way of life and urbanism as such. In this sense, they are detribalised as they adopt value systems, world views and modern scientific world order. There are noticeable differences between them and their kin groups in tribal villages.

When the rural tribal individuals improve their social and economic position mainly due to their occupations in bureaucracy or business, they migrate to Imphal, the State capital. They settle there. In first generation, they keep in touch with their rural relatives; many such families still have their shares in village land, too. The distribution of land is done by village chiefs; in many tribal settings, all the plots of land belong to the chiefs or the community. So, in order to have their share, such urban-based families do not sever all their ties with rural communities. They, occasionally, visit their original villages. From the second generation, their ties with the villages become more and more distant. They are more adapted to urban life. However, they have a feeling of using 'presentable' tribal 'material objects' so that they like to show others that they have a distinctive 'tribal identity'.

Another dimension of tribalism in Imphal urban agglomeration is the emergence of various tribal colonies. Many of them are recently established. There are only a few tribal colonies in recent past. One of the interesting features of these tribal colonies is clustering of similar tribal population in a locality or sub-locality or having a separate colony of a single tribe. These colonies are named after their tribe or in their language. Haokip Veng, Paite Veng, Hmar Veng, Poumai Colony, Nagaram, Nambulane are some of the examples of this recently developed phenomenon. With the increasing tribal population, they establish their own churches, again, named after their tribes and denominations. The tribal populations in Imphal are increasing day by day mainly due to urbanisation and its impact on the different populace in rural areas. This rural-urban migration is worldwide phenomenon. Because of this migration, Imphal, as seen in many other cities and towns, becomes cluster of villages—both tribal and non-tribal. This can be understood within the theoretical ambit of tribalism and its counter-process of detribalisation. In the existing literature, the tribalism is a social process that is observed within a tribal people.

On the other hand, we see a process of detribalisation among the middle class families. Detribalisation is meant for either, (a) moving away from tribal areas with a lapse of ties with people left behind, or (b) dropping or rejection of tribal values and behaviour pattern. In the first generation, wives are mainly from village; many of them live in their villages. From the second generation, wives from the same class are more preferred. Inter-tribal or tribe-caste marriage is also reported among the second generation middle class families. Though there is a sense of tribalism, the middle class individuals become more conscious of their class position and its expected social behaviors.

In spite of their tribalism in their unique search of spaces in governance and vast land with little density, the tribal groups face two strong challenges. First, the erosion of tribal structures due to colonial administration, emergence of middle class in post-colonial period and cultural changes brought out by westernisation and Christianity. Second, population size of each tribe is small. The Thadou, constituting about 6.64 per cent of total State population, is the largest tribe group; next is the Tangkhul commanding 5.84 per cent of total State population. Many tribes come one per cent, even below, that of the total population (Table 10:1). This demographic fact gives a way to the experimentation of formation of new identities. This is fueled by various colonial writings out of which selected texts are taken up to suit their experimentation. If some tribes are considered to come under a 'nomenclature' such as Naga, the population percentage may get pushed up to as high as 18.72 per cent of total State population. This demographic picture is the basis of post-colonial tribal politics in North East India, in general and Manipur, in particular. The politics is becoming more confusing because of the overlapping use of tribe and 'supra' tribe. For some analysis, tribes have largely ceased to exist or been irrevocably weakened (Munoz, 2010). Few anthropologists, today, would consider using the term 'tribe' as an analytical category or even as a concept for practical application (Gonazalez, 2009). Most importantly, the self-identity of an ethnic group, which has been described as "a quest for an imagined community" is much larger than a tribe (Munoz, 2010).

As their respective demographic profiles are very low, in both percentage and in number, the political struggle of each smaller tribe is practically weak. Hence, their looking for a greater identity is politically inevitable. This need of a new identity comprising of smaller tribes is

Table 10.1
Distribution of Tribal Population in Manipur

Name of the group	*Population (in number)*	*Percentage share to total Population*
Aimol	2,108	0.11
Anal	10,642	0.58
Angami	308	0.02
Any Mizo/Lushai	8,240	0.45
Chiru	6,032	0.33
Chothe	2,571	0.14
Gangte	12,793	0.70
Hmar	35,777	1.95
Kabui	62,847	3.42
Kacha Naga	33,640	1.83
Koirao	1,716	0.09
Kom	13,004	0.17
Lamkang	4,031	0.22
Mao	76,972	4.19
Maram	9,592	0.52
Maring	15,698	0.85
Monsang	1,803	0.10
Moyon	2,081	0.11
Paite	40,792	2.22
Purum	388	0.02
Ralte	250	0.01
Sema	111	0.01
Simte	8,833	0.48
Suhte	746	0.04
Tangkhul	1,07,244	5.84
Thadou	1,21,994	6.64
Unclassified Tribes	7,777	0.42
Vaiphei	26,877	1.46

(Planning Department, 2009)

fueled by the ethnic movements in neighbouring States, Mizoram and Nagaland. For this, the tribalism or even Rouch's concept of 'Super-tribalism' does not give a proper explanation. The new phenomenon can be termed as supra-tribalism which is associated with the movement for a tribal cohesion among different tribes, forming or likely to form, a new wider identity. Formation or attempt thereof of new identities by amalgamating smaller tribes is seen mainly in post-colonial Manipur.

The movement for formation of Zeliangrong by Zemei, Liangmei and Rongmei tribes, or a Naga umbrella identity or even a Kuki identity is a movement transcending the smaller tribal identities. Various political permutations and combinations among the Paite, Gangte, Zous and similar numerically lesser tribes are also seen in some localised areas of Manipur. These permutations and combinations are to evolve new identities like Zomi. The Zomi includes Paites, Vaipheis, Zous, Tedim Chin and Simtes. Though we see both ethnic fusion and fission, the emergence of new identity gives, though temporarily, strong political pressure on the existing ethnic scenario. In order to create a political space, there is always a conscious movement relating with the supra-tribalism. The supra-tribalism is observed in the political space of the Manipur; whereas the lack of cultural and social cohesion poses a greater challenge in the vector of supra-tribalism.

One of the manifestations of supra-tribalism in the State is new state-level festival organised in the name of a tribal supra-body. The *Chkavang Kut* is an age-old post-harvest festival in the Kuki world. Every Kuki village observes the festival in their lunar month of *Chavang* (November-December). The Thadous and other Kuki tribes observe the festival in their respective villages. The main part of the function is the worshipping of the deity who administered agriculture, thanking him for the yield and praying for good harvest next year too. The festival is a thanks-giving feast with songs and dances in merriment and joviality for all, in honor of the giver of an abundant harvest. After they are all Christianised, we may have the pastor in place of the priest and 'thanks-giving' done in the name of Christ. Unlike the *Kut* of pre-Christian period, which was organised in their respective village, now they drink tea in place of wine during the celebrations. The festival was forgotten for a quite sometime after all the Kuki tribes had been converted to Christianity. Since 1978, the date of the festival is fixed on 01st November. The main theme of changing face of *Chavang Kut* becomes unity, integrity, co-existence and oneness. This clearly shows the shift of cultural theme of the festival from economic and religious one to a political slogan. Traditionally, it is performed at village level with worshiping and offering to deities of their pre-Christian days who administered agriculture. Village authority decided as to when the festival would be organised in pre-Christian era. Now, the *Kut* is observed with various speeches, prayers in the name of God, fashion show and many more at selected place(s).

Likewise, the Naga political bodies try to have a common festival beyond their respective tribal boundaries so that a new cohesion may be created. Every year, since 1987, the Naga political bodies organise Lui-Ngai-Ni festival as Seed Sowing Festival on February. In order to bring out a new social solidarity, they 'invent' this super-tribalism tradition of *Lui-Ngai-Ni* (for the Nagas in Manipur to mark seed sowing festival), *Chavang Kut* (the Kukis performed as post-harvest festivals). The word Lui-Ngai-Ni is derived from three Naga tribal words, namely, Tangkhul, Rongmei and Mao/ Poumei. In Tangkhul dialect, it is derived from the word, *Luira/ Luita* which means seed sowing festival. *Ngai* is a Rongmei word which means festival and is derived from the word Gan-Ngai and *Ni* is a Mao/Poumei word which means festival. So, *Lui-Ngai-Ni* is a conglomeration of Tangkhul, Rongmei and Mao/ Poumei dialects. Any observer will notice the repetition of word meaning 'festival' – *Ngai* and *Ni.* They offer prayers to the Almighty God. It is true that every tribe in Manipur has one or another festival/ritual marking seed-sowing. Moreover, the Lui-Ngai-Ni is a festival which is organised at state-level in Manipur; this is not shared by the Nagas in Nagaland or elsewhere, meaning thereby, this is not universal among the Naga societies.

Such 'invented' traditions do not touch the spheres of village life. These super-tribalisms are not fully internalised by the villagers. These festivals are organised with a strong ideology of super-tribalism generated by the middle class. These festivals are dominated by rhetoric speeches; stage managed traditional dances and beauty pageants. The architecture of the festivals, the space arrangement, presence of dignitaries and their sitting arrangement and speeches are far from the tribal traditions. These invention have two functions (a) positive function of social solidarity of the Naga or the Kuki beyond the identities of several ethnic groups; (b) negation ideology to dominant State/National ideology which is based on State/National integration.

What is limit of the supra-tribalism? This is a point on the journey starting from tribal village to 'self-determined' state of the Nation evolved out of their post-colonial struggle. The relation between Indian nation and the tribalism or supra-tribalism has not been discussed in academic forums. One of the main questions about the supra-tribalism is how the feeling of supra-tribalism is shaped: the armed conflict prevailing in the State (region) or unequal representation in democratic processes. Is tribal militancy of North East India, a unique militancy in itself or an example of armed conflict as such? Using ethnic and tribal affiliation as root cause of conflict is misleading, because it hides the real cause for war (Paglia, 2008). In many cases of ethnic nationalism in Africa, an ethnic group is the basis for the idea of nation to be created. Anthony Smith argues in *The Ethnic Origin of Nation* (Smith, 1991), nationalism extends the scope of ethnic community from purely cultural and social to economic and political spheres; from predominantly private to public sectors. To make any real headway in the modern world, ethnic movements must stake their claims in political and economic terms as well as cultural ones, and evolve economic and political programs (Paglia, 2008). This is not the case of ethnic groups in North East India. The demographic profile of the ethnic groups in Manipur could not assert their (or of their newly emerged middle class) aspiration, the supra-tribalism is their headway to assert their political, economic and social aspirations. As there is no homogeneous or core cultural elements, they have to invent certain traditions in order to bring out a new cohesion and social solidarity. New demands for inclusion of certain ethnic groups, which were once identified with other groups (usually larger), show supra tribalism is tricky and complex phenomenon.

If we follow the line of Francis Deng, ethnic identities in themselves are not conflictual, just as individuals are not inherently in conflict merely because of their different identities and characteristics. Rather, it is unmanaged or mismanaged competition for power, wealth, or status broadly defined that provides the basis for conflict (Deng, 2000). But, the conflict at the ethnic level is being constructed on the basis of competition for power, wealth or status in the interest of emerging middle classes in 'tribal' society. In the conflict that use of supra-tribalism as its means, there are four narratives, like what is observed in Indonesia. First, complaints about economic inequality and marginalisation were commonplace under the New Order, especially in areas where the conflicts occurred. Second, there was also the feeling among the local population that their political rights and access to local power had been curtailed. Third, grievances over cultural alienation and domination were also often heard. The fourth narrative of grievance grew out of the State's violent response to the other three (Sukma, 2005). With these narratives, the tribal middle class use various mechanism including cultural similarities among different numerically lesser tribes and differences between the constructed "we" with the majority community, to construct a sense of unity or cohesion or solidarity. This situation is beyond the traditional concept of tribalism or even ethnicity; it is the supra-tribalism.

References

Daimai, K. 2011. *Land Rights of Tribal and State Land Laws.* Manipur. Imphal, www.manipuronline.

Deng, F. 2000. 'Reconciling sovereignty with responsibility'. In John W Harbeson and Donald Rothchild (Eds): *Africa in World Politics: The African State System in Flux.* Boulder: Westview Press.

Gonazalez, A. 2009. 'Going tribal — Notes on pacification in the 21st century'. *Anthropology Today* 25, 2: 15-19.

Liu, T. 2012. 'Ethnicity and tribalism in Arab transitions'. *Policy Brief.* 137: 1-5.

Munoz, A. G. 2010. *Pashtun Tribalism and Ethnic Nationalism.* Williamsburg: Tribal Analysis Center.

Paglia, P. 2008. 'Ethnicity and tribalism: Are these the root causes of the Sudanese civil conflicts?', *Africa Economic Analysis.*www.africaecomonicanalysis.org

Planning Department, G. O. M. 2009. *Population and Development.* Draft Manipur State Development Report. S. Gupta. Imphal, Government of Manipur.

Reader, D. H. 1970. 'Tribalism and detribalisation in southern and central Africa'. *Ambezia* 1,2: 55-75.

Smith, A. D. 1991. *The Ethnic Origins of Nations.* New York: Wiley-Blackwell.

Sukma, R. 2005. 'Ethnic conflict in Indonesia: Causes and the quest for Solution'. In Dusuma Snitwongse and W Scott Thompson (Eds): *Ethnic Conflicts in Southeast Asia.* Singapore: Institute of Southeast Asian Studies.

11 Ethnicity in Nagaland

Lucy Zehol

Nagaland, the sixteenth State of India, was formed on 1st December, 1963. It is bounded by Assam in the west, Myanmar on the east, Arunachal Pradesh and parts of Assam on the north and Manipur in the south. The State, as of today, consists of eleven Administrative Districts.

Naga is a generic name for a cluster of tribal communities inhabiting Nagaland, Manipur, Assam and Arunachal Pradesh and the Somra tract of Myanmar. Of the 32 such tribes,14 tribes are spread over Nagaland's eleven districts namely the Angami, Ao, Sema, Lotha, Rengma, Chakhesang, Sangtam, Konyak, Phom, Chang, Yimchunger, Khiamniungan, Zeliang and Pochury.

It needs mention here that the word 'Naga' is not indigenous to the Nagas themselves, but is subscribed by the Assamese who are the immediate neighbours of the Nagas and were one of the earliest people to have encountered them. In the historical records of the Ahoms, the word Naga was used to designate the hill people (Horam, 1975). Gradually the term was popularised and was used as a blanket term for the various tribes. At a later stage, it came to signify the identity of these people. Such a construction draws our attention to the fact that the Naga identity as such is not self-ascribed but is ascribed by outsiders.

The situation, at hand, reveals a centrifugal trend, that is, the Naga tribes are actively involved in forging a common identity that of the Naga vis-à-vis the larger Indian society and Union, contained within it is the conspicuous feature of reinforcing the discrete identities of the various tribes in one hand, while on the other is, the experience of fusion of smaller groups into forming larger identities (tribes) as in the case of the Chakhesang. During the British rule, the Chokri and the Khezha were known as 'Eastern Angami', which was ascribed by the British on the ground of cultural affinities with the Angamis, for example; practice of terrace cultivation, clothing, hair cut, food habits, etc. Beside, a close similarity between the southern Angami and the Chokri dialect is to be seen. The Chokri and the Khezha, in an attempt to break away from the Angamis, mobilised the Sangtam into forming a larger identity. Consequently, in 1978, these three groups united under a new identity known as 'Chakhesang', which is a combination of Chokri, Khezha and the Sangtam. Later in the 1980s', the Sangtams showed their apathy for this common identity and thus broke away from the Chakhesang and maintain their own separate identity as Sangtam. Nagaland thus presents a paradox, i.e., while on the one hand is the prominent effort to present a common identity, on the other, is the feature of tribals' belligerence of projecting their distinct differences.

The Naga tribes have been the subject of study of many anthropologists and others. Individually, these writing have produced many informative writings and contributed to a considerable extent towards knowledge of the Naga people. A review of the ethnographies prepared on the Naga tribes draws our attention to the absence of a comprehensive profile of the Nagas of Nagaland; the focus of attention in all the earlier ethnographies (Mills,1922, 1926, 1937; Hutton,1921; Furer-Haimendorf,1939, 1976; Smith,1925, etc.) have been confined to the description of the independent tribes. The notion of the 'Naga', as mentioned earlier, is a recent development and that, it is an inclusive term that has been imposed by outsiders, has already been stated. A comparison of the ethnographic traits is hoped to realise the cultural continuities and similarities of customs, etc., among the Naga tribes distinguishing them from others, therein gaining prominence of the discussion of ascribing a common identity to these distinctive tribes.

The present chapter is not claimed to be all embracing or conclusive. Rather, it is a tentative effort to examine the process of ethnicity in Nagaland during the pre-colonial, colonial and post-colonial periods. Ethnicity is not just a one-time event. It is also a process.

Pre-colonial and Colonial Scenario

The contemporary Naga society and their identity therein is largely resultant of the processes of change brought about by the advent of the British rule. The case of the Naga society, viewed from a historical vantage point exhibits changes in its structural make-up. An understanding of the parameters of changes requires an understanding of the traditional society of the various tribes which exhibits differences in its own merit on the basis of which the respective tribes maintains their own identity.

As evidenced by the various descriptive accounts and monographs (Mills, Hutton etc.) on the Nagas, the traditional society presents structural variations in their social and political organisations. However, a general theme appears to be operative in respect of all the Naga communities (Horam, 1975; Zehol, 1998a). The society of each of the Naga tribes is made up of crosscutting ties between the individual and the household, which is integrated into the society by being members of larger functional units; such as family, lineages, clans, age groups, youth dormitory (*morung),* localities (*khels)* and village. The individual's life style and routine of daily life is expressed through the inter-play of these social groups in operation.

It is a commonplace among the Nagas that clan membership lays on the principle of patrilineal descent. Among Naga tribes, the husband-wife unit formed the basis of all economic activity. Marriage was vital for the social advancement of the individual male for most social ceremonies depended on a man having a wife. The household was both an economic unit and a ritual unit. At a ritual level, the head of the family and his wife are responsible for the various rituals and economics that promote the well-being and the crops of the family. With the advent and spread of Christianity, all Naga tribes have accepted monogamy as the norm. Though payments of bride-wealth have virtually disappeared, some tribes are found practicing the custom though only at a ritual level to keep alive the tradition. Each of the Naga tribes has distinctive ways of life, which are of variations on certain basic social principles such as village autonomy, division into localities *(khels)* youth dormitories (*morungs*) age groups or class. They also vary according to factors such as territories, language/dialects, customs, etc.

While the readiness and ease with which the various tribes accepted the larger Naga identity may be related to the eco-political advantage, on the other, there are the shared socio-cultural ethnographic traits, which have acted as a unifying factor. It is to be stated that survey of oral traditions of the various Naga tribes; reveal similarities of ethnographic traits, which could not be coincidental.

The historian, Mackenzie, writes that the British first came into regular contact with the Nagas at about 1832. Since then, many references to the Naga have been made in their official reports as well as their tour diaries. Prior to this, any documented reference to the Naga tribes is seen to be very scanty and failing to throw much light on this early history. In the absence of reliable sources and records, we need to turn to oral traditions to reconstruct the early history of the Naga tribes.

The Naga tribes differ widely among themselves in respect of dress, language, customs, etc. However, there is an inherent similarity with the Nagas. Such assumption gains prominence and the issues involved come out with the following observation made by a Naga scholar.

> "The Tibeto-Burman speaking people of the Mongolian race that were loosely termed as 'Nagas' came from Burma and spread gradually like an irresistible tide throughout the present Naga-inhabited mountainous massifs where they entrenched themselves, preserving their customs, beliefs and languages almost intact when they found good land for cultivation and for their animals, while some of the allied tribes of the Nagas like the Karen, Kachin, Singpho, Chin Shan and others settled in Burma permanently after they had come from the western China. It is not known exactly also as to from which directions they had migrated, albeit, their tribal legends indicate the course from south to the north. Yet, it looks possible that the first wave of migrants were the Maos (Shipoumai), Angamis, Semas, Rengmas, Rongmai and Lothas who moved from the south through the mountain-fringes touching the valley of Manipur to the north. Then, they settled down at Makhriphfu, a village in Moa area near the hills of Japfu. After living there for some years, Shipoumai, now better-called Maos, settled permanently down in this area where the Maharamai or Marams closely allied to Meiteis also came in latterly, whereas the next went through different directions to different places where the Angamis, Semas, Rengmas, Chakhesangs, Zeliangrongs and

Lothas are today........ The second wave of immigrants comprised of the Ao, Changs, Kheinmunghans, Sangtams, Yimchungers and Tangkhuls............The Konyak Nagas came to their present hills from North-East of Burma" (Yonuo, 1974: 38-39).

The fact that all Naga tribes value marine articles and their folklores and legends narrate of residing near the sea or of crossing big waters indicate that they had resided near the sea or have had close association at one time with sea-faring people. The Burma Census Report (1911), mentions that successive incursions of the so-called Tibeto-Burman people from a region in western China between the sources of Yang-Tse-Kiang and Hawang-Ho were migrating ceaselessly into Burma and Assam through the river courses of Chindwin, Irrawady and Brahmaputra.

Almost all the tribes have legends and traditions that point to their sojourns in Burma and Manipur. The Angami have a tradition that tells that the Kanenoma (the Karens) tribe of Burma is their brothers; the Lotha also clearly tells of coming across a 'red earth' and crossing a river in Burma, before coming to the Manipur plains. The probable location of the Sema before they reached the Naga Hills has been shown as the country of the Khoirao tribe in Manipur whose dialect varies acutely from village to village (Hutton, 1921).

From their oral traditions, it may be assumed that the Ao, Sangtam, Chang, Phom, Yimchunger, Khiamungan and the upper Konyak have entered Naga Hills in the same wave of migration, dispersing as they moved farther west. The lack of reference in their folk tradition regarding the south westerly tribes like the Angami, Rengma, Chakhesang, Lotha, etc., except a few stay references to the Sema whose expansions got merged with the Ao, Yimchunger and the Sangtam at a few places points to this probability.

The story of the legendary village of Khezhakenoma occupies another important place in the history of Naga dispersal and migration. The Chakhesang, Angami, Lotha, Sema and the Rengma hold a tradition together that their ancestors were paternal brothers and lived at Khezhakenoma which is located in the Chakhesang area bordering Manipur (Zehol, 1998a).

The above accounts on the Naga tradition of migration and dispersal do not claim to be all embracing and exhaustive. With all said and done, the fact remains that the exact migration and origin of the Nagas is still shrouded in mystery because of lack of written records. That is why oral tradition plays an important role in trying to construct the migration and origin of the Nagas.

Before the advent of the British, the Naga tribes were living in permanently settled villages, high above the hills separated from each other by the rough terrain and inter-feuds. They did not develop a conscious Naga nationalism until much later. In most early literature, the Naga villagers are depicted as an independent, isolated, autonomous political entity. Though it virtually appeared as such, there existed networks of alliances and patronages linking of several villages. However, such alliances occur only within the villagers of the same tribe.

The Konyak provide a prime example of such alliance with their powerful villages under the chiefs (*Angs*) and their satellite villages, forming a cluster of inter-dependent villagers. The powerful Angami village of Khonoma, Kohima and Viswema also had their own satellite villages. This, however, did not necessarily involve political dominion.

In the days of head hunting and feuds, such alliances served the purpose of mutual aid. It also provided with a certain amount of political cohesion. Organisation of this order above the village level was only a matter of temporary alliance. Over-arching political organisations, which could settle disputes between villages and which could act on behalf of the tribe as a whole in dealing with outsiders did not seem to have existed.

In 1825, when the Burmese invasion into Assam was halted, and Assam was annexed following the treaty of Yandaboo (1826), the British began looking for alternative means of communication between Assam, Manipur and Burma, in order to safeguard their territory and check the frequent raiding. The two spheres of British interest became joined on Naga territory. The most obvious and shortest route lay through the Naga Hills, and in 1832, Captain Jenkins and Pemberton entered the Naga Hills through the Angami territory in an attempt to survey the possibilities.

In 1879-80, several Angami Naga villages united against the British occupation, which culminated in the Khonoma war. After this Naga uprising, a shift in policy towards the Nagas can be observed. The Regulating Act of 1880 'excluded' the Nagas from the operations of the enactments relating to civil and criminal procedures, through which their indigenous laws and customs were hoped to remain unaffected as much as possible and British administration kept to a minimum. However, the fact was that the British had a strong presence. The Naga Hills were divided into two sub-divisions (Kohima and Mokokchung) where a deputy commissioner and additional deputy commissioner and their subordinate officers were stationed. The administration sought to work through indigenous people in which can be seen the combination of the two policies of indirect rule. This policy functioned through two mechanisms: at the village level, *Gaonburas* (village elders/headmen) were appointed from among the various clans of the village as per the traditional customs, who worked as mediators between the village and the British rulers. The *Gaonburas* or G.Bs, as they were popularly known was incorporated into the village council that continued to function in as much the traditional way even today. The British continued their hold over the independent villages through the *Gaonburas* who were given power to arbitrate any local disputes on behalf of the British. They were given red shawls as a symbol of their position.

At the district level, *Dobashis* (interpreters) were appointed and attached to the district officers' courts. The *Dobashis* assisted the British officers by interpreting the customary laws in arbitrating the disputes and issues brought to them. They wielded much governmental powers and proved to be the pillars of the British administration. They were given arbitrary powers to act on behalf of the British officers, through whom they could extend their powers and authority even to the un-administered area to some extend: "local chiefs and headmen, who were called command *Dobashis* and paid by Government, acted on his behalf and reported major incidents which required attention" (Elwin, 1969: 28).

The colonial rule was rife with series of changes. Inter-village raiding and head hunting was prohibited in the administered area. As the line of 'administered area' expanded further into the hills and more of the scattered Naga villagers were brought under, the aggregation of power on a wider and consolidated scale was affected through the institutions of the *Gaonburas* and the *Dobashis;* uniting the Nagas under a single political power, which hitherto had never existed.

Though the British strategy of administration was to allow the continuation of the autonomy of the villages and traditional custom; in effect, it was instrumental in breaking down the customary powers and authority of the chiefs and the village councils over the village citizens, by providing a higher authority (above the village) to which aggrieved party could appeal.

The Cross-followed the British flag (missionaries). Horam (1975) observed that, "the Naga religious abounds in taboos and Christianity also laid down strict rules as to what was to be done and what was to be left undone. Converts change of faith means mere exchange of one set of taboos for another".

The primary object of the missionaries was to spread the gospel. Yet, they had a strong determination to enlighten the people through education. This is seen in the mission workers carrying out their educational projects wherever they went. So much so, that the mission centers grew into important centre for education. The mission centre at Kohima was an important educational centre, to which students from all over Naga areas were known to come for studies. The amount of good that Christianity brought is apparent; however, the cultural decay by the abandoning of traditional religion cannot be ignored. As a consequence of Christianisation, traditional ceremonies and rituals and sacrifices were abandoned as they were considered symbols of paganism.

Contained in this is the fact that the missionaries have been the offenders in suppressing Naga culture as it finds expression in their songs and their dances. "Singing and dancing among the Naga tribes were originally associated with head-hunting and therefore religious ceremonies were the chief targets of attack by Christian missionaries and every convert to the new faith was to have nothing to do with them. This, at first, dealt a very severe blow to the most beautiful and colourful aspect of Naga culture. Recently however, the folly of destroying their own culture has been brought home to the tribes and fortunately genuine attempts are being made for the revival of these practices" (Horam, 1975: 122).

By the turn of the century, the educated Christian Nagas with jobs under the Government was set up as the role model of the ideal life constituting the elite section of the emerging Naga society.

Christianity did have its positive effects. Beside its civilising influence, it was instrumental in generating and opening new avenues for social mobility. Achievements with education came up with the loosening of the walls of the traditions and the widening of the horizon of the people beyond the barriers and limits of the village life. English language and Christianity transcended both village and tribal isolation and brought the people of the different linguistic groups into permanent contact.

The educational centers provided a ready base for inter-tribal contact and recognition of each other as belonging to the same indigenous category (Naga) as against outsider (non-Naga). It was instrumental in opening of new avenues of social contact and mobility; opportunity for non-traditional mode of social achievement in the form of white collared jobs under the colonial set-up. All along, the growth of urban centers to serve the needs of the colonial administrative requirements provided a contact zone for the various tribes at different levels.

Urban centers/townships became important multi-ethnic centers where businesses and administrative set-up created new social classes, different from those in the villages. The social prestige of wealth gained through the hosting of the feast of merit was displaced by the new economic trend of the urban rich. This generated a general inclination of the people towards urban life style and achievements thereby leading to the decline of traditional isolation and wider contact. Simultaneous to this, the new market-oriented economy also attracted outsiders in increasing numbers seeking jobs and business avenues; consequent to which competition for the opportunities emerged.

The Naga identity, being ascribed by outsiders, was not known or popular among the people and it was not in general use among the Nagas till recently.Even as late as 1954, the people of Tuensang district rarely spoke of themselves as 'Naga' but as Konyak, Chang, Phom etc. (Elwin, 1961). The British rulers and the American missionaries were responsible for popularising the notion of the 'Naga' term to the outsiders and even among the Nagas themselves. Today, the term by which they were known to the outsiders provide a common identity to the otherwise discrete tribes, which has, became their rallying point.

This idea of a common Naga identity was crystallised through the movement of sovereignty that caught momentum on the eve of the colonial rule in India. The British, by taking over the Naga inhabited region, affected political and administrative centralisation. The centralisation of power resulted in increased interaction where the discrete tribe came into greater and closer contact with stranger-tribes and discovered commonalities for the first time that had not been evident earlier.

Ethnicity in respect of the Nagas may be observed as an activated response to the colonial process. The development of Naga ethnicity was consequently crystallised through the Naga movement. The Naga movement was a political movement, which at a later stage, took a military turn. From the start, this was much counterpoised to the larger Indian society than to British colonialism. It was feared that under free India, the Nagas will not be allowed the same freedom and protection which they enjoyed under the British. In the midst of the political turmoil, brought upon by the Indian freedom movement and the evident transfer of power, the growing fear and apprehension found expression in the form of advocating Naga freedom and complete independence in the emerging free India. It was a political move. The Nagas did not participate directly in the Indian freedom movement and that the Naga issue figured very negligibly in the Indian political scenes was explicit. The Naga movement for sovereignty sought to gain political prominence for the Nagas as a nation. Naga ethnicity, which essentially was motivated as a consequence of socio-cultural need to distinguish Nagas as a distinct identity, is thus seen as a major mobilising factor to highlight and accentuate the political aspirations and interests of a distinct group of people who see them as a peripheral group within a larger Indian (Hindu) society. The Naga movement, which was largely political and military, and Naga ethnicity, a social-cultural phenomenon resulting out of the colonial process are seen complementing the cause of the other.

Post-colonial Scenario

At the critical juncture of Indian independence and the withdrawal of the British, which gave the Nagas a measure of special protection in respect of their traditional rights and customs and the Christian religion, Naga leaders were apprehensive of losing their distinctive identity. Consequently, under their influences, their collective fears and apprehensions found expression in their striving for Naga solidarity.

The feeling of discontent since the imposition of the British rule reached a climax in the post-independent period. This was much activated by the political aspirations of the rising new elite of the emerging Naga society. Thus, the ethnic upsurge in Nagaland is seen as a reaction to the forceful occupation of their lands by the British and later incorporation with India.

In the wake of the formation of the Nagaland State, the Centre embarked on a phase of programs to develop the State as well as to dampen the Naga separatist movement. Despite all this, on one hand the Naga nationalistic movement has not lost its momentum; rather, it has come in direct conflict with the Centre. On the other hand, the Centre has created a condition of under-development, new inequalities and economic disparity among the various tribal groups. In accordance with the delusive assumption that tribal societies are homogenous, which has been inherited from the colonial writings, it is assumed that any State help or efforts to develop the tribal areas will be equally shared.

However, the individual members receive the major portion of the welfare benefits. As such, no homogenous society can remain open to receive additional benefits, privileges that come from outside for some of its members, and still maintain its homogeneity. Logically, it is the upper stratum of the population who benefits most from the socio-economic privileges given to the tribal communities. It is the advanced tribes like the Angami, Ao, Lotha, Rengma and Sema who get more advantages out of the developmental programmes than the backward tribes like the Chakhesang, Chang, Khiamniungan, Konyak, Phom and Sangtam as a consequence of their more representation in the policy formulating agencies. All these processes ultimately enhance the gulf between the various tribes and between the tribal rich and poor; nullifying the many purpose of the developmental efforts.

In the dawning of the new era of social development and transformation, the Naga tribes find themselves horizontally stratified owing to organisational and technological development as a result of being enveloped into the developmental process. The development package and the unequal distribution entailed each tribe into competition between themselves and with the rest of the larger nation-society for the socio-economic privileges and the welfare benefits it accrued. In the process of this, the expression of their ethnocentrism is projected and the essential traditional identity found re-interpretation as a competitive mechanism in all spheres of economy, politics and social relations.

Conclusion

What is observed is that the ethnic Naga groups in Nagaland are involved in a constant process of conflicting interaction of projecting their differences and distinctions from one another, in contrast to their collective effort of forging a unified pan-Naga identity. Ethnic boundaries may change but ethnicity as a mechanism of social mobilisation will persists unabatedly in Nagaland.

References

Alemchiba, M. 1970. *A Brief Account of Nagaland.* Kohima: Naga Institute of Culture.

Elwin, V. 1961. *Nagaland.* Shillong: NEFA Research Department.

Elwin, V. 1969. *The Nagas in the Nineteenth Century.* p. 28, Bombay: Oxford University Press.

Furer Haimendorf, C.V. 1939. *The Naked Nagas: Head Hunters of Assam in Peace and War.* London: Mehuen and Company Ltd.

Furer Haimendorf, C.V. 1976. *Return to the Naked Nagas: An Anthropologist's View of Nagaland.* Delhi: Vikas Publishing House.

Horam, M. 1975. *Naga Polity.* p. 122, Delhi: B.R. Publishing Corporation.

Hutton, J.H. 1920. *The Sema Nagas.* London: MacMillan.

Hutton, J.H. 1921. *The Angami Nagas.* London: MacMillan.

Mackenzie, A. 1884. *The Northeast Frontier of India.* Delhi: Mittal Publication.

Mills, J.P. 1922. *The Lotha Nagas.* London: MacMillan.

Mills, J.P. 1926. *The Ao Nagas.* London: MacMillan.

Mills, J.P. 1937. *The Rengma Nagas.* London: MacMillan.

Smith, W.C. 1925. *The Ao Naga Tribe of Assam: A Study in Ethnology and Sociology.* London: MacMillan.

Yonuo, A. 1974. *The Rising Nagas: A Historical and Political Study.* pp. 38-39, New Delhi: Vivek Publishing House.

Zehol, L. 1998. *Ethnicity in Manipur.* New Delhi: Regency Publication.

Zehol, L. 1998. *Women in Naga Society.* New Delhi: Regency Publication.

Index